Promises
OF
HOPE

JILL LOWRY

ISBN-13: 978-1-737-18251-1

Promises of Hope

Cover & Scripture Images Designed by Kerry Prater. Interior Design by Katharine E. Hamilton

To all who believe in the power of prayer.

INTRODUCTION

Hope begins with a relationship with our Heavenly Father though His Son, Jesus Christ. Once you have this eternal relationship, renewed hope grows inside you through the indwelling power of the Holy Spirit.

This enlightened hope will open the eyes of your heart to see in ways you never thought possible. Only God, through His Son, Jesus and the Holy Spirit, can help you see this way. Your eyes will see His light the more you spend time with Him in prayer.

Has it been a while since you prayed?

Have you made prayer a part of your daily routine?

Prayer is an open line of communication between you and the Lord. It is a place where you can grow your hope and communicate your love to Him.

Open this book and read the daily promise from God. Then read the prayer and pray it silently or out loud each day. This is a start for you to grow your prayer life. As you pray His promises and make prayer a priority, you will find more hope for each day. God is waiting to hear from you. Yes, He wants to hear you pray. Open your heart and pray the promises of God!

...having the eyes of your hearts enlightened, that you may know what is the hope to which he has called you, what are the riches of his glorious inheritance in the saints...

EPHESIANS 1:18

January 1

*"And I will ask the Father, and he will give you
another Helper, to be with you forever."*
John 14:16

My Prayer

Dear Heavenly Father,

Thank You Father for Jesus
Christ who You gave to us
so that we can be forgiven
and have eternal life with
You. We have been saved
by Your grace. And when we
believed and asked Jesus to be our
Savior, we received the gift of another
Helper, the Holy Spirit, to be with us
forever! We praise You, Lord, for these precious and
special gifts! What a joy it is to know the Holy Spirit
dwells within us! He is not only our Helper, but He is
also our Comforter, Constant Companion, Teacher,
Advocate, and Voice of Truth. His powerful presence
in us gives us hope, peace, and joy, forevermore! We
are blessed by Your overwhelming love and blessed
by Your powerful Spirit!

In Jesus' name,
Amen

January 2

"Let the words of my mouth and the meditation of my heart be acceptable in your sight, O LORD, my rock and my redeemer."
Psalm 19:14

My Prayer

Dear Heavenly Father,

Help me to speak what is pleasing and acceptable to You, O Lord. I aim to please You with what I say. Give me boldness to keep living out my faith without wavering! I know this is what You desire for me. I am thankful I can spread the fragrance of Your love as I live out what You desire for me. I am humbled by Your blessings over me and honored to be able to pray to You, my Redeemer! You have saved me from sin and given me opportunities to speak with newfound love. I will trust You forever and live eternally grateful, my Lord!

In Jesus' name,
Amen

January 3

"For I, the LORD your God, hold your right hand; it is I who say to you, 'Fear not, I am the one who helps you.'"
Isaiah 41:13

My Prayer

Dear Heavenly Father,

Thank You for helping me with my fear. When I am afraid, I put my trust in You! I am so thankful You have held my hand and guided me in the right direction. I will not let fear stop me from the destiny you desire for me. I know Your hand of protection and guidance is upon my life. You lift me up right when I need You. Thank You for reminding me that I will hear You as I call upon You, seek Your will and truth from Your Word, and pray bolder and bigger prayers— All with unrelenting faith!

In Jesus' name,
Amen

January 4

His Promise

*"God, the Lord, is my strength; he makes my feet like
the deer's; he makes me tread on my high places."*
Habakkuk 3:19

My Prayer

Dear Heavenly Father,

I am stronger with You, Lord, for any challenge I
face! You give me extra courage just when I need
help. As I call upon You, I am filled with renewed
strength. You have given me hope as I lean closer on
You and rely on Your promises. My faith is built on
solid ground because I am trusting You as my Rock. I
am leaping with joy as I stay in step with You! I will
not give up but will keep believing with passion and
running with endurance the race set before me!

In Jesus' name,
Amen

January 5

"Then you will call upon me and come and pray to me, and I will hear you."
Jeremiah 29:12

My Prayer

Dear Heavenly Father,

I am calling upon You, my Lord. Help me as I pray. I need courage and strength. I know You will answer me when I lift up my prayers to You with a thankful heart. Your healing is just a faithful prayer away. I am falling on my knees with a humble heart asking for a miracle. I know You are capable of the impossible! I will keep rejoicing in hope, being patient in tribulation, and being constant in prayer. I will keep calling upon You and lifting my prayers up to You, my Provider and Protector. Thank you for attending to the voice of my prayers. You are able!

In Jesus' name,
Amen

January 6

His Promise

"How long, O Lord? Will you forget me forever?
How long will you hide your face from me?"
Psalm 13:1

My Prayer

Dear Heavenly Father,

I love You, O Lord!! You have been so faithful to me! Even in the waiting, I know You are working. Help me to be patient and trust You as I wait for your answer. Your timing is always perfect, so I will continue to trust and not doubt. My faith will be my eyes when it is time to see! Until that moment in time, I will praise You and remain faithful and obedient. As I delight more in You, the question of 'how long?' becomes, "how can I be more devoted to You?"

In Jesus' name,
Amen

January 7

"I lift my eyes to the hills. From where does my help come? My help comes from the LORD who made heaven and earth."
Psalm 121:1-2

My Prayer

Dear Heavenly Father,

Thank You for protecting me as I lift my eyes to You. I know my help comes from You, my Lord! You can do anything You please. Nothing is impossible for You! I have seen miracles as I have trusted in You. You have brought new life to me. You have restored me to a place of peace. I am clinging to Your truth and life as I trust You wholeheartedly, my Lord, my Protector! I will keep my eyes always fixed upon You as I keep believing in Your promises!

In Jesus' name,
Amen

January 8

"All Scripture is breathed out by God and profitable for teaching, for reproof, for correction, and for training in righteousness."
2 Timothy 3:16

My Prayer

Dear Heavenly Father,

Thank You for the truth in Your Word that You breathe out. I have grown closer to You as I hold these truths in my heart. You look for the faithful and obedient who will humble themselves before You, seek Your truth, and live out Your instructions. I am listening and will obey. As I pray, I am clinging to this truth found in the Word of Life. Your promises give me hope. Your Word brings me peace. Your presence gives me joy. I can face anything when I abide in You and live by Your Word. It is alive and active within me!

In Jesus' name,
Amen

January 9

"Every good gift and every perfect gift is from above, coming down from the Father of lights with whom there is no variation or shadow due to change."
James 1:17

My Prayer

Dear Heavenly Father,

You are the giver of every perfect gift! Thank You for each gift that has come down from You. The greatest gift You have given us is Jesus Christ who gives us eternal life. Because of Him, we can live in freedom and peace. By His stripes, we are healed. Through His blood, we are saved from our sins. By His love, we are made whole again. Because He lives, we can face tomorrow. This new life is ours in Jesus Christ!

In Jesus' name,
Amen

January 10

"You shall love the LORD your God with all your heart and with all your soul and with all your might."
Deuteronomy 6:5

My Prayer

Dear Heavenly Father,

Oh, how I love You, Lord! I am devoted to You with all my heart, soul, and mind. I will put You above all else, which is what you desire. I will finish the work You have called me to do, even when it gets tough, or others may give up. I know You will never leave me. I want to know You more, my Lord! I want to be able to share everything with You. I need to hear Your will for me. I yearn to discover the calling that You have given me. I live to please You, wholly devoted and determined as Your beloved child! I am Yours forevermore!

In Jesus' name,
Amen

January 11

*"And my God will supply every need of yours
according to his riches in glory in Christ Jesus."*
Philippians 4:19

My Prayer

Dear Heavenly Father,

Oh, how I love You, Lord! I know You supply all of
my needs in Christ Jesus! I am not doubting— But
trusting! This contentment gives me hope as I watch
You work all things out, powerfully and wonderfully,
as You always do. I trust You when I cannot see. I
believe You when I do not understand. I hope when
all seems impossible. I have faith the size of a
mustard seed. What a joy it is to worship and praise
You with a thankful heart! You are so good all the
time!

In Jesus' name,
Amen

January 12

"With long life I will satisfy him and show him my salvation."
Psalm 91:16

My Prayer

Dear Heavenly Father,

Thank You for the hope that You give me as I hold fast to my salvation. Your promises have enlightened and encouraged me. I am free because You have saved me. I am strong because You dwell within me. I am hopeful because You love me. I am infused with power and truth from Your Spirit and Your Word. I am looking upward with thanksgiving for Your treasures in Heaven. My hope of glory reigns as I praise You for eternal life that is mine in You! I will not stop rejoicing and singing praises to You, my Lord of salvation!

In Jesus' name,
Amen

January 13

*"Return to the LORD your God, for he is gracious
and merciful, slow to anger, and abounding in
steadfast love."*
Joel 2:13

My Prayer

Dear Heavenly Father,

Your grace has saved me! Your
love is lavished upon me with
grace upon grace. I believe, Lord.
It is Your amazing grace that gives
me hope once again! I am alive
with You, my Savior, for it is for freedom that you set
me free. I am forgiven by You, my Redeemer. I am
strong and courageous because of You, my Refuge. I
am loved abundantly by You, my Rock. I am restored
by You, my Healer. In You, I am worthy and wanted.
I will walk in love and live with grace as I return to
You with all of my heart!

In Jesus' name,
Amen

January 14

"Your word is a lamp to my feet and a light to my path."
Psalm 119:105

My Prayer

Dear Heavenly Father,

You brighten up my world, O Lord! As I listen to truth from You and Your Word, I am enlightened and encouraged. You speak to me as I listen. When I pray, I cling to You and Your promises. My faith is centered directly on You. I hear promises from Your Word of life and I am empowered. I have faith the size of a mustard seed that grows as I trust and obey each one. Your light shines brightly on me as I remain engaged with You in Your powerful Word and Spirit of Truth!

In Jesus' name,
Amen

January 15

"Christ in you, the hope of glory."
Colossians 1:27

My Prayer

Dear Heavenly Father,

I have renewed hope in You, O Lord! The hope You give brings life and peace. As I cling to this hope, I am alive again! You are faithful. Since I have a relationship with You, I have everything I need to find hope. In the darkest days, Your light guides me to hope. In the brightest moments, I see evidence of Your hand upon me. Your never-ending hope surrounds me and I know You will help me all the time! Your glory reigns in me as I cling to hope on my journey. With You in me, there is always hope of glory!

In Jesus' name,
Amen

15

January 16

*"Call to me and I will answer you, and will tell you
great and hidden things that you have not known."*
Jeremiah 33:3

My Prayer

Dear Heavenly Father,

I am ready to hear the deep and hidden things You are
wanting to tell me. I know You will speak as I seek
You. I am praying with an obedient heart to hear what
You have called me to do. I am ready to follow Your
lead and let go of my fear. It is well with my soul as I
engage with You and let You enlighten me. My
obedience to You will show You my love and faith.
Thank You for speaking truth to me. I am listening to
You and will eagerly open the eyes of my heart Lord
to discover more!

In Jesus' name,
Amen

January 17

"If God is for us, who can be against us?"
Romans 8:31

My Prayer

Dear Heavenly Father,

I am relying upon You, my Lord. You are with me making me courageous as I face these challenges. I will let You lead me where there is hope and purpose. I have new courage as I step out and face the world with You. With Your power, I can run with endurance the race set before me. With Your spiritual strength, I can see with Your eyes of faith as I press on. I know there is nothing that can stop me when You are protecting, encouraging, and guiding me! I am secure in You, my Lord and Defender. I am strong and brave!

In Jesus' name,
Amen

January 18

"Let us hold fast the confession of our hope without wavering, for he who promised is faithful."
Hebrews 10:23

My Prayer

Dear Heavenly Father,

I have living hope with You, Lord! I will hold tight to this hope as I keep living and walking the path you've set before me. You will remain faithful as You have promised me! I am claiming all Your promises and I will not fear when You are near to me. I will be strong and brave when facing unknowns or feeling lost. I feel hope when I am blessed by You, my Lord. I am praying for wisdom and direction as change comes my way. I have even more hope as I let the Holy Spirit strengthen me and encourage me each and every step of my journey. I am holding fast to hope without wavering because You are my living hope, active and alive in me!

In Jesus' name,
Amen

January 19

"Lead me to the rock that is higher than I."
Psalm 61:2

My Prayer

Dear Heavenly Father,

I need strength because I am weary. You are the rock I can cling to as I seek to be courageous, strong, and wise. As I draw closer to You, I will listen to Your voice and let You lead me. I will act obediently and fearlessly with Your Spirit in me. I am enriched with Your powerful love and redeeming grace, and I am thankful for Your mighty blessings over me. I can live with power and freedom when I live under the comfort of Your wings of protection and purpose. Praises to You, my Lord, my rock and salvation!

In Jesus' name,
Amen

January 20

"Restore us, O LORD God of hosts!
Let your face shine that we may be saved!"
Psalm 80:19

My Prayer

Dear Heavenly Father,

I need the restoration that only comes from You, Lord. You have deposited the Holy Spirit within me to bring me closer to You. You have entrusted me with this amazing gift! Oh, how I need You more and more! I cherish all the spiritual blessings You have graciously given to me. Thank You for loving me like You do. I am secure knowing You comfort and direct me. I am praying for the fire of rebirth inside me to keep burning brightly and for it to spread to those around me. I am sure You will bring more positivity and passion to me as I dwell with You. I am loved and wholeheartedly devoted to You, my Lord!

In Jesus' name,
Amen

January 21

"The eyes of the Lord are in every place, keeping watch on the evil and the good."
Proverbs 15:3

My Prayer

Dear Heavenly Father,

I am fully awakened to Your voice, my Lord! You make me strong and courageous as I cling to You today. I feel peace when I let go of my burdens and take hold of You. I know You have been waiting to set me free! I am the one who has been hesitating and worrying instead of trusting You fully. Now that I have come home to You, I have rediscovered my joy! My heart will heal as I stay devoted to You. Thank You for watching over me, protecting me from harm, and guiding me. Here I am, Lord, determined and devoted!

In Jesus' name,
Amen

January 22

"But for you who fear my name, the sun of righteousness shall rise with healing in its wings. You shall go out leaping like calves from the stall."
Malachi 4:2

My Prayer

Dear Heavenly Father,

I am ready for healing in Your name, my Lord! There is power in the name of Jesus. I believe in Your healing power over me. I am strengthened and encouraged when I trust You as my strong tower. I will not fade or fear with You by my side. I will know Your will as I trust and obey Your promptings. I will listen and rise with healing when You speak truth over me through Your Word. Thank You for enriching my life. I trust You with all my heart! I am leaping with joy!

In Jesus' name,
Amen

January 23

"For the gate is narrow and the way is hard that leads to life, and those who find it are few."
Matthew 7:14

My Prayer

Dear Heavenly Father,

You are the only way that leads to life. As I enter through the narrow gate by trusting Your way, I will be blessed with confidence. It is in this path that I see Your promises come to be. I am secure in You as I walk by faith and not by sight. I see with spiritual eyes as I engage with You. I can see clearly now that the scales have been removed from my eyes! My heart is healed by Your power and through Your presence! My soul is renewed with utmost joy and gladness! Thank You for giving me faith to live fearlessly so I can be counted as one of the few!

In Jesus' name,
Amen

January 24

"He who calls you is faithful, he will surely do it."
1 Thessalonians 5:24
My Prayer

Dear Heavenly Father,

I know You will do what You promise because You are faithful. I am blessed to know Your love and feel Your peace. As I pray today, I know You are able and will take care of me. I have all that I need with You, my Lord. Your grace will come alive in my heart as I trust You. I know there are greater things ahead when I listen and obey You. I see Your faithful hand over me and let Your faithfulness infuse me with greater strength and courage! My aim is to love in such a way that I am continually faithful to You!

In Jesus' name,
Amen

January 25

His Promise

"The prayer of a righteous person has great power as it is working."
James 5:16

My Prayer

Dear Heavenly Father,

I am sure You hear my prayers and I know You will answer me. I will keep praying for what is on my heart with faith knowing that You are able, Lord. I am eagerly awaiting the fulfillment of Your promises to be revealed. I have hope even though I do not yet see. I am walking by faith and not by sight and am praying for Your will to be done. As I am still before You, I know that You are the God who provides all that I need. Thank You for faithfully loving me like only You can do! I will keep praying earnestly believing great things will happen!

In Jesus' name,
Amen

January 26

"You shall love the Lord your God with all your heart and with all your soul and with all your mind."
Mathew 22:37

My Prayer

Dear Heavenly Father,

You are so amazing, Lord! I love You with all my heart, soul, and mind. I am so thankful and so blessed by Your love. When I seek more of you, I feel Your never-ending love and remarkable grace deep in my soul. I am touched tenderly by Your grace and love. I know You are working mightily in me as I rest in Your presence. Every day with You abiding in Your love is better than the day before! Your promises encourage and enlighten me. I hear You, O Lord, and I will trust and obey You all the way!

In Jesus' name,
Amen

January 27

"Those who sow in tears shall reap with shouts of joy!"
Psalm 126:5

My Prayer

Dear Heavenly Father,

I know You are the way to joy! Even in the heartache, my joy from You is here to stay. Even as I weep, the joy deep in my heart cannot be taken away! I am leaning on You, Lord Jesus. In these trying days, there is still hope to be experienced. In Your presence, there is fullness of joy and at your right hand are pleasures forevermore. I will keep choosing joy as I stay close to You, my Lord. You are my bright light in the darkness!

In Jesus' name,
Amen

January 28

His Promise

"Having the eyes of your hearts enlightened, that you may know what is the hope to which he has called you, what are the riches of his glorious inheritance in the saints."
Ephesians 1:18

My Prayer

Dear Heavenly Father,

Thank You Lord for giving me refreshing hope! I know You are the one who will enlighten me with truth when I trust You wholeheartedly. You will show me the way to go when I listen, look, and live out my faith. The scales will fall off my eyes to see You as I surrender and let You work in me. You will strengthen me with hope as I let You lead me. I am grateful for Your blessings! Thank You for Your glorious riches! I am alive with faith and awakened with hope!

In Jesus' name,
Amen

January 29

"I will bless the Lord at all times; His praise shall continually be in my mouth."
Psalm 34:1

My Prayer

Dear Heavenly Father,

Oh, how I honor You, my Lord! Your praise shall continually be in my mouth! Thank You for attending to the voice of my prayers. I know You hear me and will answer. All I have to do is keep praying with faith for what is on my heart. I know You hear me, Lord, and I believe You are greater than any problem. You promise to help me overcome my weakness, grief, and loss. You always do what You promise! I am trusting You even when I do not understand because I know You are faithful!

In Jesus' name,
Amen

January 30

"The Lord will keep you from all evil;
he will keep your life."
Psalm 121:7

My Prayer

Dear Heavenly Father,

Thank You for promising peace. As I guard my heart, You will give me strength. As I come closer to You, I feel encouraged and loved. In Your presence, I have a perfect peace that cannot be explained. All is well when I surrender and let You come closer to me. You keep me protected and peaceful. Nothing can take away this love and peace You give me. There is no way I can be separated from Your love. Your love remains. Your peace provides. I have all that I need in You!

In Jesus' name,
Amen

January 31

His Promise

"And I am sure of this, that he who began a good work in you will bring it to completion at the day of Jesus Christ."
Philippians 1:6

My Prayer

Dear Heavenly Father,

You are so wonderful, my Lord! I know You will help me as I keep moving in Your direction. I will serve You as You have called me. I will complete the work You have purposed for me. In this world, there are multiple paths I can take, but I will choose the way that leads to You and life everlasting. All the paths without You lead to defeat. But You, O Lord, are for me and will be my eternal guiding light! I am healed in Your presence!

In Jesus' name,
Amen

To them God chose to make known how great among the Gentiles are the riches of the glory of this mystery, which is Christ in you, the hope of glory.

COLOSSIANS 1:27

February 1

His Promise

"Wait for the Lord; be strong, and let your heart take
courage; wait for the Lord!"
Psalm 27:14

My Prayer

Dear Heavenly Father,

I will wait for You, Lord! As my heart embraces courage, I feel Your hand upon me. I am praying for strength and healing as I patiently wait. You are always there for me, even when I do not understand why I must wait. Thank You for helping me. I love being close to You, my Lord. It is in the stillness of my soul where I feel Your peace. As I dwell in Your presence, I am finally at rest and do not need to know why. Instead of questioning and doubting, I will trust You to show me Your perfect way!

In Jesus' name,
Amen

February 2

His Promise

"Rejoice with those who rejoice,
weep with those who weep."
Romans 12:15

My Prayer

Dear Heavenly Father,

I am praying for an encouraging peace to share with those who are hurting. Help me to comfort those who are suffering with the comfort You have given me. Even through the tears, I can feel Your comforting peace. I know You weep with those who weep because You feel our pain. And when others rejoice, I will rejoice with them as well! It is so good to be able to share joy with those who are rejoicing and to be happy for those people who are blessed by You! Thank You, Lord, for the peace and joy you freely give. I will rejoice again and again with hope and give comfort to those who need it, because You comforted me!

In Jesus' name,
Amen

February 3

His Promise

"For God gave us a spirit not of fear but of power
and love and self-control."
2 Timothy 1:7

My Prayer

Dear Heavenly Father,

You want me to remain in Your love. As I activate the power of the Holy Spirit inside me, Your power guides me. As I live in Your love, I will turn away from fear and draw closer to the power of the Holy Spirit. Every moment is refreshing in Your presence. I will take captive every thought and make it obedient to You, Lord— obedient to Your Word and Spirit. I will not let fear enter my heart. For I am Your beloved, and instead of fear, I will ground myself upon Your power and love and the encouragement it brings me. As I let this love reside in me, Your light will overcome any darkness and beautiful rays of hope will shine through. Your love is rejuvenating and so beautiful to me!

In Jesus' name,
Amen

February 4

"And he awoke and rebuked the wind and said to the sea, 'Peace! Be still!' And the wind ceased, and there was a great calm."
Mark 4:39

My Prayer

Dear Heavenly Father,

I will continue hoping for peace even when I cannot see because I know You are there for me. Even when anxiety tries to creep in, I feel Your peace. In moments of doubt, I remind myself of Your promises and peace fills my soul once again. As I trust You, my heart is enlightened with new found joy and my soul is strengthened with courage. I will keep praying earnestly with a grateful heart as I hear You say, 'Peace! Be still.' Thank You for Your peace. It is well with my soul!

In Jesus' name,
Amen

February 5

His Promise

"The Lord is my shepherd; I shall not want."
Psalm 23:1

My Prayer

Dear Heavenly Father,

Thank you for being my comforter and my provider. I know I can call on Your name and You will be there. As I come to You in my struggle, I feel at peace knowing you can hear me. Just when I need You, a light of hope from Your love sparks in my heart. You give me eternal love that enlightens my soul. I am blessed and grateful for all Your blessings upon me! I am certain of this hope. It resides in my heart. Here I am, Lord, I shall not want because I have all that I need in You, my Shepherd!

In Jesus' name,
Amen

February 6

"For nothing will be impossible with God."
Luke 1:37

My Prayer

Dear Heavenly Father,

I know nothing is impossible with You. I will trust and obey You and this will sustain my hope and faith. As I trust, You speak. As I obey, You work inside me. My faith will grow as I keep my eyes fixed, not on my understanding, but on You. Time and time again I will be tested, and I want You to find me faithful. I want to rise with wings like eagles as I wait upon You. Even when I am weak, I will keep walking in the direction You take me. I will be encouraged to go because Your promises are true, and Your power is real. Nothing is impossible with You, my Lord! I believe!

In Jesus' name,
Amen

February 7

"And the peace of God shall guard your heart and your mind in Christ Jesus."
Philippians 4:7

My Prayer

Dear Heavenly Father,

I feel Your peace, O Lord, as I come closer to You and let You guard my heart and my mind. Even in this storm, there is perfect peace. Even when I have no words, You comfort with me with the touch of Your presence inside my soul. Even with my broken heart, I feel Your peace— The peace that passes all human knowledge and understanding. As I say goodbye once again to my loved ones who are seeing You, Lord, I cannot help but feel peace knowing they are with You. I grieve for loss, but not as one without hope! My hope is in the promise that one day we will all meet in Heaven. I know I will be reunited with my precious loved ones who are rejoicing with You right now! What a promise I have with You, my Lord, my Living Hope! One day I will meet You face to face and my faith will be my eyes! Hallelujah!

In Jesus' name,
Amen

February 8

"When the Spirit of Truth comes, he will guide you into all the truth, for he will not speak on his own authority, but whatever he hears he will speak, and he will declare to you the things that are to come."
John 16:13

My Prayer

Dear Heavenly Father,

Oh, how I love Your blessings over my life. I am thankful for the gift of the Holy Spirit You have given me. As I draw closer to You, I feel You guiding me with Your outstretched hand. Your Spirit is upon me helping me navigate these waters. I am full of peace and life as I look to You, my Helper. I will be fully connected to the Spirit when I stay surrendered to You. Your love has showered me with perfect peace. I will continue to walk in the Spirit, my Lord! Life in the Spirit is the only way I will choose to live. I have opened and received my gift!

In Jesus' name,
Amen

February 9

"Our help is in the name of the LORD, who made heaven and earth."
Psalm 124:8

My Prayer

Dear Heavenly Father,

You are my refuge and strength and a very present help in trouble. Oh, Lord, thank You for helping me. I need You every moment to direct me and comfort me. In Your presence there is peace and healing. I am praying for guidance, my Lord. When I am in Your presence, I feel Your blessed peace all over me. Holy Spirit, cover me and help me. I am weak and need more courage and strength for this challenge I'm facing. I need You, Lord!

In Jesus' name,
Amen

February 10

"Not everyone has faith. But the Lord is faithful."
2 Thessalonians 3:2-3

My Prayer

Dear Heavenly Father,

Thank You for Your faithfulness, O Lord! I know You are always faithful to me. Even when I cannot see, You are there guiding me to truth and encouraging me to believe. I will walk with eyes of faith and a heart filled with hope. It is in Your mighty presence I draw my strength to face my giants. I will not fear them when You are near to me. I will trust You through it all knowing Your faith will be carrying and comforting me every step of the way. In You alone, my Lord, I do faithfully trust!

In Jesus' name,
Amen

February 11

His Promise

"Keep your heart with all vigilance, for from it flow the springs of life."
Proverbs 4:23

My Prayer

Dear Heavenly Father,

I know You want me to guard my heart. I come to you and listen with love. I open my spiritual eyes to see, hear, and touch what You share with me in Your Word through love. I know You love me, so I will love You with all my heart, soul, and mind. Every part of me is awakened to You when I pray. Your presence is before me showing me the ways to love You more! I will guard my heart against this world, for it is Yours! Help me to listen to the Spirit calling me to greater blessings in life with You. I am alive and awakened to new life with Your love strengthening my soul, enriching my mind, and renewing my heart!
I love You, my Lord!

In Jesus' name,
Amen

February 12

"In your righteousness deliver me and rescue me;
incline your ear to me, and save me!"
Psalm 71:2

My Prayer

Dear Heavenly Father,

Lord, I need You! I know You will rescue me and save me from the trouble surrounding me. I am thankful Your ear is inclined to my prayers! I will keep lifting them up one by one. I know if I ask You, the answer will come in Your will and Your timing. You delight to hear Your children pray and seek Your will. You listen to each prayer, and You deliver those who come to You. I believe and receive all Your promises of redemption. You have reached, rescued, and restored me, Lord! I am saved by your gift of grace, and it is well with my soul!

In Jesus' name,
Amen

February 13

"And walk in love, as Christ loved us and gave himself up for us, a fragrant offering and sacrifice to God."
Ephesians 5:2

My Prayer

Dear Heavenly Father,

Thank You for Your sweet aroma of love that infuses me as I look to You. I am blessed and excited to be Your follower, to spread Your fragrance wherever I go. Thank You for loving me and sharing Your love with me. I will walk in Your love and share my heart with those You put in my path. I am eager to see Your plans for me to come to life as I stay connected to the Spirit. You are my strength, my portion, and my song all the day long!

In Jesus' name,
Amen

45

February 14

"So then let us pursue what makes for peace and for mutual upbuilding."
Romans 14:19

My Prayer

Dear Heavenly Father,

I will pursue peace, my Lord as I keep close to You and Your promises to me. As I rest in the fold of Your peace, I am strengthened once again. Thank You for building me up and nurturing me so that I can encourage others. In Your presence, there is life and peace. I am living in peace and standing on Your promises. In this world there is heartache and trouble, but when I give You my burdens and take up Your yoke, I will find the perfect peace You promise me!

In Jesus' name,
Amen

February 15

*" 'Yet even now,' declares the Lord, 'return to me
with all your heart, with fasting, with weeping ,and
with mourning."*
Joel 2:12

My Prayer

Dear Heavenly Father,

I hear You, Lord, and will return to You. I have
listened to You in the night calling me to come closer
to You. There is much for me as I let You embrace
me with Your love. In the trials of this world, I know
I have a friend cheering me on to keep going. That
friend is You, my Lord, my Redeemer! I am full of
joy and peace because I know You love me so much
that You want my whole heart so I can be revived
with new life again! I love You and will follow You,
Lord Jesus wherever You lead me!

In Jesus' name,
Amen

February 16

"I am he who comforts you; who are you that you are afraid of man who dies, of the son of man who is made like grass."
Isaiah 51:12

My Prayer

Dear Heavenly Father,

We need You, O Lord! Thank You for promising to comfort us. There is so much heartache around us and we are saddened by what we see. These times we live in are challenging and we are tired, weary, and have forgotten You. Forgive us for being selfish and faithless. We humbly come to You and ask for strength and new life again. We know that only You can provide all that we need. Help our unbelief and give us courage and comfort as we press on! There is hope found in You as we draw closer to Your love and grace!

In Jesus' name,
Amen

February 17

"If anyone is in Christ, he is a new creation. The old has passed away; behold the new has come."
2 Corinthians 5:17

My Prayer

Dear Heavenly Father,

You have given me new life as I have believed and surrendered my heart to You. I am overwhelmed by Your resurrection power that has transformed me! I have let go of the old and have let You breathe new life into me. I have said "yes" to Your love and mercy and "no" to defeat and doubt. I am created to live in Your love and spread Your joy and peace. I believe You have so much to show me as one of Your children. I will open my eyes to see beyond myself and will listen to Your voice to hear You speak truth to me. I am a new creation in Christ!

In Jesus' name,
Amen

February 18

His Promise

"For truly, I say to you, if you have faith like a grain of mustard seed, you will say to this mountain, 'Move from here to there' and it will move, and nothing will be impossible for you."
Matthew 17:20

My Prayer

Dear Heavenly Father,

I believe! You have said that my faith will grow as I keep trusting You. Even the smallest faith can move mountains! There is hope when I believe and walk by faith and not by sight. I have hope in what I cannot yet see because I am clinging to You by faith. You have promised and I believe what You have proclaimed. Thank You for this amazing new life that is mine in You. I know I will see miracles because You have said I will, and Your words are true. I am devoted to You, my Lord, and I believe with a heart of great faith!

In Jesus' name,
Amen

February 19

"I am the LORD who made all things, who alone stretched out the heavens, who spread out the earth by myself."
Isaiah 44:24

My Prayer

Dear Heavenly Father,

You are powerful and amazing! I see You in everything You have created. How can I thank You enough for who You are to me? You have brought life to me and have given me courage to stand firm. You have helped me navigate my ups and downs by being present in my life. You remind me of Your power and glory when I look at what You have created with Your outstretched hands. Your promises are real and have revived me. I live in the light of Your love. I know I can do all things through You, my Lord, as You constantly strengthen and encourage me to faithfully press on with Your eternal love and grace upon me!

In Jesus' name,
Amen

February 20

"And we know that for those who love God all things work together for good, for those who are called according to his purpose."
Romans 8:28

My Prayer

Dear Heavenly Father,

Oh, how I love You! I am grateful You work all things out for my good according to Your infinite plan. I know You will do what You say because You are faithful! Even when I cannot see the details, I trust and know I am secure in You. My confidence is found in You alone. I trust You and my faith is found in only You, Lord. I will keep my eyes fixed on You and nothing else. As I lean on You, my security is real and wonderful. Your peace blankets me in warmth and peace. When I feel it, I know it is You and I am thankful! Peace be still, my soul!

In Jesus' name,
Amen

February 21

"And when they had prayed the place in which they were gathered together was shaken, and they were all filled with the Holy Spirit and continued to speak the word of God with boldness."
Acts 4:31

My Prayer

Dear Heavenly Father,

I will keep speaking boldly with the Holy Spirit in me. Thank You for giving me this power that continues to grow stronger as I seek more of Your presence. I will continue growing as I let You work in me. There are blessings waiting to be shared with others as I let You direct me to them. I want to encourage these people with Your love as I speak truth and show them kindness and patience. With renewed faith, I can continue this path. I will not grow weary of doing good, and with You empowering me, will keep speaking and building others up. I am filled with joy for the journey!

In Jesus' name,
Amen

February 22

"Restore us, O God; let your face shine,
that we may be saved!"
Psalm 80:3

My Prayer

Dear Heavenly Father,

Save us and restore us. Shine upon us, O Lord! We hunger for You and know that You can bring restoration to our lives. In this world we can become weary and worn out from all the deadlines and demands. But You, O Lord, will give us new life as we trust You and seek You with our whole hearts. We are ready for a fresh wave of revival in our souls. Fill us and use us to build Your kingdom as You desire. As we are filled with the Spirit and serve You, we will see restoration in our hearts and joy will flood our souls! Help us to live in renewed fellowship with You each day!

In Jesus' name,
Amen

February 23

"All these with one accord were devoting themselves to prayer together with the women and Mary the mother of Jesus, and his brothers."
Acts 1:14

My Prayer

Dear Heavenly Father,

I am devoted to You, my Lord. As I pray today, speak life and peace to me. I will keep lifting up my prayers to You, O Lord, as I know You hear me and will respond. My faith grows with every prayer from my heart. I will continue to pray together with others as You desire. Thank You for answering us as we keep faithfully praying. Without faith, it is impossible to please You. But You, Lord, are faithful to us and love to hear the prayers of Your people as we pray from our hearts!

In Jesus' name,
Amen

February 24

"Sanctify them in the truth; your word is truth."
John 17:17

My Prayer

Dear Heavenly Father,

Help me to speak and live out the truth as I seek more of You each moment. I hear Your voice speaking truth to me when I read Your Word and write it on my heart. I feel Your presence as I continually pray. The path to take is clear when I meditate on Your Word. I will be free when I surrender my sins and burdens through confession and ask You for forgiveness. You are ready to bless me with a new life full of grace as I listen, trust, and obey. My aim is to love with a sincere heart full of faith that flows from You, my Lord. I know the truth of Your love. And I know with certainty that this truth that is only found in You will set me free!

In Jesus' name,
Amen

February 25

His Promise

"May he grant you your heart's desire and fulfill all your plans!"
Psalm 20:4

My Prayer

Dear Heavenly Father,

Oh, how I thank You for fulfilling the plans You have for me! As I delight in You, I know the desires of my own heart even more. These plans are exactly what You have chosen for me. You have blessed me with a close connection with You and the people You place in my life. I am grateful for each blessing and promise You give to me. As I praise You, I am alive with great joy. I know I am Your beloved whom You shower with the light of Your glory and grace that will shine forever!

In Jesus' name,
Amen

February 26

His Promise

"And God was doing extraordinary miracles..."
Acts 19:11

My Prayer

Dear Heavenly Father,

Oh, how I love You and need You, Lord! You have promised me so much and I believe in You. You are the God of the impossible who performs extraordinary miracles all the time. I am full of praise today as I pray. I thank You for who You are and how much You love me. I see evidence of Your goodness all over my life. I am praying in the Spirit and with Your power to see even more miracles. Show me Your glory, Lord!

In Jesus' name,
Amen

February 27

"Weeping may tarry for the night, but joy comes with the morning."
Psalm 30:5

My Prayer

Dear Heavenly Father,

I have joy as I ponder the promises You give me. You have blessed my life with wonderful joy that remains in me no matter what problems or difficult circumstances come my way. I have put You first and You have given me more joy than I can ever describe. I am joyful for Your presence in me. I am stronger as I lift my prayers to You, my Lord. My tears from yesterday have turned to shouts of joy today because You are so faithful! Thank You for reminding me that I will have endless joy when You remain in me!

In Jesus' name,
Amen

February 28

*"As each has received a gift, use it to serve one
another, as good stewards of God's varied grace."*
1 Peter 4:10

My Prayer

Dear Heavenly Father,

Thank You for gifting me with spiritual gifts so I can
serve. I am eager to use these gifts for Your glory.
You have blessed me abundantly and I am joyfully
privileged to work for Your kingdom. I will join You
in the work You are already doing around me. I will
fervently continue to share the message of hope that
comes from You. I will walk with You in strength
and power. I will keep my eyes fixed on
You and the work You have called
me to do. Joy blossoms in me
and those around me as I
serve You!

In Jesus' name,
Amen

We have this as a sure and steadfast anchor of the soul, a hope that enters into the inner place behind the curtain...

HEBREWS 6:19

March 1

"Rejoice in hope, be patient in tribulation, be constant in prayer."
Romans 12:12

My Prayer

Dear Heavenly Father,

I am so thankful for You, my Lord! I rejoice for all You are doing in my life! You are constantly holding me up. In the stillness of my soul, You are there giving me hope. When the unexpected problems of the world surround me, You give me peace. When I do not understand, I will rejoice because I know You are my Lord who will never let me go. Your presence in my heart brings me feelings of safety and security. I will keep praying, be patient in waiting, and continue rejoicing for who You are to me. I know nothing is too hard for You! Therefore I will trust You even more as I pray with a grateful heart of praise!

In Jesus' name,
Amen

March 2

"Therefore take up the whole armor of God, that you may be able to withstand in the evil day, and having done all, to stand firm."
Ephesians 6:13

My Prayer

Dear Heavenly Father,

I am so thankful for Your armor that I can put on for protection and power. I will stand firm with strength and faith knowing that You will help me. I will not fear evil, but will proactively and faithfully pray to You, my Lord! Thank You for being an ever-present help in trouble. You are my Rock of refuge in this storm. I have hope when I wake up to more of Your endless love that comforts me. I know You are surrounding me with courage as I stand firm. I am able to withstand because I am embellished with my whole armor!

In Jesus' name,
Amen

March 3

"The heart of man plans his way, but the LORD establishes his steps."
Proverbs 16:9

My Prayer

Dear Heavenly Father,

I know You will show me the way as I let You establish my steps. I have new hope as I reach out to You and let You lead me. I am most grateful for Your plan because You want the best for me and will give me a hope and a future. There is no wrong way to go when I make the choice to obey You. I know Your blessings will come as I hold them one by one. I have unexpected joy even in the struggles because You are with me every moment. I hear You, Lord, and will trust You for Your plan even when I do not understand!

In Jesus' name,
Amen

March 4

*"Therefore let us be grateful for receiving a kingdom
that cannot be shaken, and thus let us offer to God
acceptable worship, with reverence and awe."*
Hebrews 12:28

My Prayer

Dear Heavenly Father,

I am grateful for You and will worship You. I know Your Kingdom cannot be shaken and this truth brings me hope. Even in the toughest times, You are there for me and I am at peace. I will walk with renewed hope as I trust You wholeheartedly. I lift up my prayers believing You will answer. There is joy just knowing You, Lord. I need You in my life to guide and direct me, O Lord. Awaken me to new life and revive me again so that I can see with fresh faith!

In Jesus' name,
Amen

March 5

His Promise

"Be still and know that I am God."
Psalm 46:10

My Prayer

Dear Heavenly Father,

I am so grateful for You, my Lord! You have promised me peace when I trust You with my whole heart. As I sit still and meditate, I can hear You say, "Peace be still." My heart is flooded with Your perfect peace, the peace that is present even in the midst of the division and strife in this world around me. It is in the stillness of my soul, that I see You and hear You. I know that You are present with me. Thank You for being there for me always!

In Jesus' name,
Amen

March 6

"Look carefully then how you walk, not as unwise but as wise, making the best use of the time, because the days are evil."
Ephesians 5:15-16

My Prayer

Dear Heavenly Father,

I will make the best use of my time seeking You. I will listen and obey the plan for me. Even when I cannot see all the details, I will trust You and not let doubt enter my heart. It is time to live out what I believe by putting faith first. As I draw closer to You, Your plan becomes clearer with each step I take. Your wisdom comes to me as I encounter You in Your Word. I am carrying hope in my soul as live out Your promises!

In Jesus' name,
Amen

March 7

"I know your works. Behold, I have set before you an open door, which no one is able to shut."
Revelation 3:8

My Prayer

Dear Heavenly Father,

I am thankful for the open door you've set before me. I will confidently walk through it toward the ministry you've called me to. Through Your Word You encourage me to be mindful of the direction You wish for me to go. With Your Spirit in me, I will spread the light of Your love, Lord. I can walk with power and strength as You fill me with more of Your Word and Spirit every day. It is my joy to be a co-laborer with You, Lord. The fields are ripe for the harvest for more people to be saved. Help me to see the people I can serve and help bring closer to You!

In Jesus' name,
Amen

March 8

"O LORD, you will ordain peace for us, for you have indeed done for us all our works."
Isaiah 26:12

My Prayer

Dear Heavenly Father,

Even in these storms, I will run to you! Especially when I am afraid, I will seek Your peace. You rescued me when I surrendered my thoughts, words, actions, and will to You. I breathe easy in peace when I lay down my selfishness and let Your Spirit come to life in me! I am not afraid of the turmoil I see around me, but I believe in the peace that You promise me and all who believe! There is hope for peace, but only if peace is found in You!

In Jesus' name,
Amen

March 9

"Casting all your anxieties on him,
because he cares for you."
1 Peter 5:7

My Prayer

Dear Heavenly Father,

I will cast my burdens and worries upon You, my Lord! You have helped me see that I am holding on to things I need to surrender and release. You will take all those concerns from me if I choose to give them to You. I will let go and receive Your help. It feels amazing to have Your peace and healing when I let go and let You lead me. Your plan is perfect, and I see that now. I am thankful and humbled by Your presence and promises over me. In the stillness of my soul, I am waiting on You and living in peace!

In Jesus' name,
Amen

March 10

*"Behold my servant, whom I uphold,
my chosen for whom my soul delights."*
Isaiah 42:1

My Prayer

Dear Heavenly Father,

Thank You for upholding me! I know You are pleased when I choose to delight and serve You. You have called me and given me the purpose to love You and see with kingdom eyes. You want all Your children to stand up for truth and be a beacon of light for others to see. I will join You in the work You are already doing. I see, Lord, with a kingdom heart, and I do believe I am loved and chosen by You!

In Jesus' name,
Amen

March 11

"And awe came upon every soul, and many wonders and signs were being done through the apostles."
Acts 2:43

My Prayer

Dear Heavenly Father,

O Lord, I am in awe of You and Your blessings upon my life! You remind me daily of the blessings you've given me by showering me with Your covenant of love that shines brightly in the heavens. After the storm, You reveal Your promises. I see the wonder and glory of who You are when I gaze in awe and praise at who You are to me. Thank You for giving me Jesus so that I can find the joy that comes from knowing Him personally! I am full of Your joy, which lasts forever! The greatest blessings come from You, Lord! Thank You for Your goodness, love, and grace upon me!

In Jesus' name,
Amen

March 12

*"But you, beloved, building yourselves up in your
most holy faith; and praying in the Holy Spirit."*
Jude 20

My Prayer

Dear Heavenly Father,

I praise You, Lord, for my great faith. I feel renewed
as I cling to You and obey Your commands. You
promised me the Holy Spirit when I believed, and I
feel Your presence inside me. I will listen to Your
still, small voice and draw closer to You as I pray
faithfully and fervently. You are holy and wonderful,
Lord! In Your presence there is
fullness of joy and perfect peace
for me. It is well with my soul
as I pray in the Holy Spirit and
wholeheartedly trust You!

In Jesus' name,
Amen

73

March 13

"Therefore do not be anxious about tomorrow, for tomorrow will be anxious for itself. Sufficient for the day its own trouble."
Matthew 6:34

My Prayer

Dear Heavenly Father,

I will trust You and quit worrying about tomorrow. You know what is best for me and will always help me with whatever comes my way. You do not like to see me fret and worry about the future. Instead, You desire that I trust You and keep my faith. You have plans for me, a future and a hope that surpass my imagination. I will walk by faith and let You show me the path. As I commit my plans to You by trusting and believing, hope will enter my soul and my worries will fade away. I am free when I surrender all and let You lead me!

In Jesus' name,
Amen

March 14

His Promise

*"For where your treasure is,
there will your heart will be also."*
Luke 12:34

My Prayer

Dear Heavenly Father,

Your steadfast love is so wonderful and fulfilling, my Lord! Your treasure is what I seek as I soak up Your love in my heart. Thank You for giving me hope once again. I put my faith in You, Lord, and focus on what really matters— A closer relationship with You. As I sit in Your presence, I bask in the light of Your love. I feel You touching my heart even more as I pray for Your peace and healing. It is so refreshing to see You working all around me. I will join You in what You are calling me to do as I keep looking to You, my Lord, and treasure, the heavenly things above that last forever!

In Jesus' name,
Amen

March 15

His Promise

"Let the one who boasts, boast in the Lord."
1 Corinthians 1:31

My Prayer

Dear Heavenly Father,

Thank You for who You are to me! I am grateful and full of thanksgiving for all You have brought to my life! You are the one who showers me with joy and covers me with hope. I have abundant life because I have a deep relationship with You. Without You, I would not know this true peace in my life. This is a peace the world cannot give to me. It is a perfect and praiseworthy peace beyond human comprehension, and it is there even during the most difficult times. You are everything to me! I will praise You forever and lean on Your promises, boasting of Your glory forever. You are my all in all!

In Jesus' name,
Amen

March 16

"For the mountains may depart and the hills be removed, but my steadfast love shall not depart from you, and my covenant of peace shall not be removed, says the LORD, who has compassion on you."
Isaiah 54:10

My Prayer

Dear Heavenly Father,

Your peace is so calming to me. Your steadfast love fills my soul. I am basking in this place of peace and love You give as I come closer to You. Even with trouble all around me, I have Your perfect peace alive inside me. It is refreshing to be still in Your presence. When I am still before You, nothing else matters as Your peace flows through me and Your love touches me. It is well with my soul when I am with You! Just give me Jesus!

In Jesus' name,
Amen

March 17

"The righteousness flourish like the palm tree and grow like a cedar in Lebanon."
Psalm 92:12

My Prayer

Dear Heavenly Father,

Oh, how I love You, my Lord! As I trust You more, You radiate from me. I feel the warmth of Your love as I listen and obey. You want the best for me. As I follow You and do what you say, I flourish. I have endurance as long as I continue on the path of righteousness with You. I am awakened with greater hope as You strengthen me for any challenge that comes my way! Just like the palm tree, I will stand strong and tall with life flowing inside me directly from You. In Christ, I am alive!

In Jesus' name,
Amen

March 18

"But seek first the kingdom of God and his righteousness, and all these things will be added to you."
Matthew 6:33

My Prayer

Dear Heavenly Father,

I am opening my heart to seek You, Lord! You have given me renewed hope. I aim to seek You first in my life. In the morning, I rise with strength and courage because I have Your love, Lord, and this fills me with even more hope to face the day. I have eyes to see You, Lord, when I faithfully pray about everything. My direction is clear when You are my focus. I can hear Your voice guiding me into all truth as I set my heart on You. With You, I have the wisdom I need in my life. Blessings abound as I abide in You and see Your glory and Your righteousness come to life!

In Jesus' name,
Amen

March 19

<u>His Promise</u>

"Return to me with all your heart…"
Joel 2:12

<u>My Prayer</u>

Dear Heavenly Father,

I am praying for more faith in all that comes my way. As I stretch my faith in all circumstances, You will do more inside my heart. I am confident that You will make all things new again as I return to You with my whole heart. I am secure when I stay close to You, Lord. I am content when I let go and let You work in me. I am at peace when I put you first in my life. I am whole when I put faith first and follow You closely and wholeheartedly!

In Jesus' name,
Amen

March 20

"May mercy, peace, and love be multiplied to you."
Jude 2

My Prayer

Dear Heavenly Father,

I need You, Lord! You continually shower me with more peace, mercy, and love. I feel You comforting me as I pray today. There is so much on my heart. I give it all to You, Lord. I will cast all my burdens on You so that You can take them and wholly restore me. Thank You for listening to my prayers and loving me like You do. I am fully Yours, ready for the healing, my Lord and Savior! I pray, knowing You will provide all that I need!

In Jesus' name,
Amen

March 21

*"For all the promises of God find their Yes in him.
That is why it is through him that we utter our Amen
to God for his glory."*
2 Corinthians 1:20

My Prayer

Dear Heavenly Father,

Oh, how I thank You, Lord, for Your glory! You are mighty and wonderful, and my heart knows You very well. I am saved by Your grace and embraced by Your love in abundance. I have seen You in all and over all. There is evidence of Your goodness all over my life. I have hope as I live connected to You. I praise You as I look to the heavens and give thanks. Thank You for showering me with spiritual blessings from above. My heart is Yours, my Lord. I say Amen as I ponder all Your promises to me!

In Jesus' name,
Amen

March 22

His Promise

"But the Lord stood by me and strengthened me, so that through me the message might be fully proclaimed."
2 Timothy 4:17

My Prayer

Dear Heavenly Father,

You give me extra strength as I lean on You. I am strong with You when I am weak. It is so amazing to know Your love that remains, restores, and rejuvenates me! Loving and living with You has not only given me strength but has opened my heart to believe in the impossible! I know You are able! You are the God who makes a way when there seems to be no way. "With You" all things are possible! I do believe!

In Jesus' name,
Amen

March 23

"Without faith it is impossible to please him, for whoever would draw near to God must believe that he exists and that he rewards those who seek him."
Hebrews 11:6

My Prayer

Dear Heavenly Father,

You want to see my faith. You yearn for me to stay faithful. I want to please You, Lord, so I will put my feet to faith and show You my faith is alive and growing. My heart is devoted to You, and I live by faith, letting You work in and through me. When I am weak, You give me strength. When I am unsure, You give me renewed hope. When I am blind, You restore my vision. When I am lost, You comfort me and show me the way back to You. I am faithfully Yours!

In Jesus' name,
Amen

March 24

*"O God, you are my God; earnestly I seek you;
my soul thirsts for you; my flesh faints for you, as in a
dry and weary land where there is no water."*
Psalm 63:1

My Prayer

Dear Heavenly Father,

O Lord, how my soul thirsts for You, my living water! You have filled me up and restored me with Your Spirit. I am renewed day by day as I draw from Your wellsprings of life. Your love and grace have brought peace and joy to my soul. I am full of thanksgiving and hope for what lies ahead for me. I keep You "with" me wherever I go. Your blessings fall upon me when I stay close to You. I will be still and let You refresh me with Your living water flowing in and through me!

In Jesus' name,
Amen

March 25

*"Set your minds on things that are above,
not on things that are on earth."*
Colossians 3:2

My Prayer

Dear Heavenly Father,

I am praising You for Your eternal love and grace! I am so blessed to have a relationship with You, my Lord. When I give you my whole heart, You give me hope. I am stronger with You present in me. I am wiser with Your truth alive in me. I am healthier with Your love in me. I am redeemed with Your grace upon me. I am restored with Your Spirit active in me! Your treasures are what I seek! Hallelujah!

In Jesus' name,
Amen

March 26

"Now faith is the assurance of things hoped for, the conviction of things not seen."
Hebrews 11:1

My Prayer

Dear Heavenly Father,

I am earnestly seeking You and Your will for me. I know You want me to have faith and continue believing. Thank You for the plan You have for me even the parts that have not been revealed yet. I will keep pursuing You as I grow in faith. I have purpose with Your power as I surrender and let You lead me into all truth. My faith increases as I trust You even more. You open my eyes of faith when I let go of self and surrender all. You are my reward!

In Jesus' name,
Amen

March 27

*"Behold, I will bring to it health and healing,
and I will heal them and reveal to them abundance of
peace and truth."*
Jeremiah 33:6

My Prayer

Dear Heavenly Father,

Thank You for Your healing promises. I believe what You tell me. I don't understand all the details of why I must go through the struggle, but I do know You are able to heal me. I grow a little bit stronger each day as You hold me. Your love for me comforts me through the pain. In my darkest time, You are my light. I will keep the faith as I stand on Your truthful promises. You are the same today, yesterday, and forever and Your steadfast love never changes. I receive Your calming and healing peace over me as I pray.

In Jesus' name,
Amen

March 28

His Promise

"For you have need of endurance, so that when you have done the will of God you may receive what is promised."
Hebrews 10:36

My Prayer

Dear Heavenly Father,

Thank You for making a difference in my life! When I believe what You say and put my full faith in You, I receive extra endurance for the journey ahead of me. I am wiser and stronger when I depend wholeheartedly on You. Only You can defend me and give me the courage I need for any challenge. As I face adversity, Your strength will take me to new heights and Your promises will come to life. There is power in the name of Jesus! Hallelujah, I am free!

In Jesus' name,
Amen

March 29

"For the gate is narrow and the way is hard that leads to life, and those who find it are few."
Matthew 7:14

My Prayer

Dear Heavenly Father,

I want to be one of the few who keep on Your road. I will diligently keep my eyes on You and Your will for me as I walk by the Spirit. I will commit my way to You so You can infuse me with strength and power for the journey. I will run my race with endurance as I press on through the challenges. You are my hiding place along my journey and a very present help in trouble. The peace You give me is so powerful and fulfilling when I stay the course with You. I am overflowing with faith and eternally encouraged by You, my Lord, as I drink of Your living water. I will walk closer to Your love each day as I keep You first in my life and stay on Your road to life. As I follow You, I will be blessed indeed!

In Jesus' name,
Amen

March 30

"I waited patiently for the LORD,
he inclined to me and heard my cry."
Psalm 40:1

My Prayer

Dear Heavenly Father,

I will wait patiently for You as I pray. Thank You for bending down to listen to my heartfelt prayers. You know what I need even before I ask You. It is so good to be able to call upon You whenever I need You and know You will be there for me. Your love is so amazing! The Holy Spirit has rejuvenated and restored me to new life! I am full of praise. I am growing closer to You in the waiting. I am devoted to You even more with each prayer I lift up to You, my Lord. O my soul, how I love You!

In Jesus' name,
Amen

March 31

*"Delight yourself in the LORD and he will give you
the desires of your heart."*
Psalm 37:4

My Prayer

Dear Heavenly Father,

Oh, how I love to delight in You! As I spend more time with You, I receive more of Your blessings of devotion. You are so wonderful, Lord! As I listen and obey, You give me the everlasting joy that remains. My heart is full of the bountiful love You give me. My soul is on fire for You as I dwell in Your presence. I will keep delighting in You and Your promises with praise on my lips!

In Jesus' name,
Amen

Let us hold fast the confession of our hope without wavering, for he who promised is faithful.

HEBREWS 10:23

April 1

"Therefore, since we are surrounded by so great a cloud of witnesses, let us also lay aside every weight, and sin which clings so closely, and let us run with endurance the race that is set before us."
Hebrews 12:1

My Prayer

Dear Heavenly Father,

Thank You for giving me endurance to run this race set before me. I am hopeful for what lies ahead because I have You with me. I am never running alone, but have extra strength with You before, beside, and behind me with each step I take. I choose to fix my eyes on You and not my circumstances. I will let go of fear and hold on to faith because I know You give me power and perseverance. I am ready to run to You, Lord Jesus!

In Jesus' name,
Amen

April 2

"Be kind to one another, tenderhearted, forgiving one another, as God in Christ forgave you."
Ephesians 4:32

My Prayer

Dear Heavenly Father,

You ask me to forgive as You have forgiven me. You want me to be kind and compassionate. I will listen and obey. I will forgive those who have hurt me, Lord. I have let go of all my frustrations toward those who disappoint me. I will move forward with compassion and love in my heart because that is what You desire. My soul feels liberated as I do what pleases You. I am made new as I let you permeate every part of me. I am alive with new hope as I follow You to freedom and walk in the light of Your love!

In Jesus' name,
Amen

April 3

His Promise

"For it is God who works in you, both to will and work for his good pleasure."
Philippians 2:13

My Prayer

Dear Heavenly Father,

Oh, how I thank You, Lord, for the work You have given me. I will work for Your will to be done. As I trust and obey, You will show me the way. I work to please You, my Lord. As I face each challenge, infuse me with power for what lies ahead. I do trust You through all of life's challenges. All that I do will be for Your glory as I work and surrender all to You at this moment. I can do all things through You who strengthens me. Work mightily in me!

In Jesus' name,
Amen

April 4

"Continue steadfastly in prayer,
being watchful in it with thanksgiving."
Colossians 4:2

My Prayer

Dear Heavenly Father,

I will keep praying because I know You will answer me, Lord! As I continue praying, You will respond. You need me to remain steadfast in my faith as the answers are coming. I will wait upon You with hope in my heart. I am eager to see what You will do as I trust, obey, and pray. I love knowing You want the very best for me! You saved me by grace when I said yes to Your love. I give You all my heart, Lord, so You can do Your will in me! I love You!

In Jesus' name,
Amen

April 5

"Be filled with the Spirit."
Ephesians 5:18

My Prayer

Dear Heavenly Father,

I will continue, moment by moment, to live in the Spirit as You fill me. My focus and my prayer are You, O Lord. I need You, O Lord. Your Spirit gives me life and peace. I am overjoyed to know this joy that comes from You. My life is blessed when I stay focused and connected to You, Lord, my power and life source. As I pray, I am encouraged and grateful for the relationship I have with You. It grows deeper as I am filled with the Spirit, live in the Spirit, and listen and obey the Spirit. Holy Spirit, You are welcome and wanted!

In Jesus' name,
Amen

April 6

His Promise

"And I am sure of this, that he who began a good work in you will bring it to completion at the day of Jesus Christ."
Philippians 1:6

My Prayer

Dear Heavenly Father,

I will keep working because You have called me until the day of Jesus Christ. I will press on to serve as You wish. I will believe You for greater blessings. I see what You want to do in me, Lord. Today and every day, I strive to be used more for Your kingdom purposes. I cannot wait to see what You will do as I keep doing good works for You, my Lord. I am blessed to be able to use my gifts for Your glory today and forever! I am called by You, justified by grace, and glorified in Your presence, O Lord!

In Jesus' name,
Amen

April 7

His Promise

"Therefore, if anyone is in Christ, he is a new creation. The old has passed away; behold, the new has come."
2 Corinthians 5:17

My Prayer

Dear Heavenly Father,

In You, I am made new! The old has passed away and the new has come. I am refreshed and alive in Your presence, my Lord! I am stronger with Your mighty hand upon me. I can do all things through You who strengthens me! I will live in freedom because I have new life and peace. I will remain in Your peace as I stay close to You. I will have faith as I walk in the Spirit. As I grow in grace and knowledge, my thoughts, feelings, and actions will be in unison with You and Your will for me. I am walking by faith and not by sight in my new life in Christ!

In Jesus' name,
Amen

April 8

"Though you have not seen him, you love him. Though you do not now see him, you believe in him and rejoice with joy that is inexpressible and filled with glory."
1 Peter 1:8

My Prayer

Dear Heavenly Father,

I love You, Lord! I praise You with great joy and a grateful heart for loving me! I am worthy of Your love because You call me beloved. I am special to You. Even when I cannot see, I believe in all Your promises and am standing on each one. Thank You for loving me and for always being with me, even when I mess up. I receive Your grace in my life and have renewed hope as I stand in your love. I love being close to You. There is fullness of joy filled with glory in Your presence, my Lord!

In Jesus' name,
Amen

April 9

*"The LORD is near to all who call on him,
to all who call on him in truth."*
Psalm 145:18

My Prayer

Dear Heavenly Father,

Thank You for being near to me. I know You are near to those who call on You in truth. I am calling on You, my Lord. I want to draw closer to You and hear You speak to me. I will not fear but will keep looking up. It is so good to be close to You! I will lift my prayers to You as I listen to Your voice to hear truth. Other voices will try to discourage me, but You, O Lord, will always encourage me! I have set my hope on You, my loving God full of mercy and grace!

In Jesus' name,
Amen

April 10

*"From the same mouth come blessing and cursing.
My brothers, these things ought not to be so."*
James 3:10

My Prayer

Dear Heavenly Father,

I know You want us to bless others with our mouths.
You need us to be encouragers by our words and
actions. You know what we need to do to make a
difference. You know the hope we need as we keep
walking by faith with our eyes on You. We need to be
patient and kind so that others may experience Your
love. This world needs more love, kindness, and
grace. Let us be those who reach others with Your
love and share joy. As we bless others, we will all
beautifully bloom because it is more blessed to give
than to receive!

In Jesus' name,
Amen

April 11

His Promise

"Peace to you!"
Luke 24:36

My Prayer

Dear Heavenly Father,

You want peace for me! I will look to You and see peace. I will cling to You and Your promises and find even more peace. I will wait upon You and find my path to peace. In You, I will have *perfect* peace. I see You in the flowers that bloom so beautifully. I feel You in the wind that blows gently on me. I hear You when the birds sing to me. I know Your calming peace as I rest comfortably in Your loving arms. I receive Your peace, Lord!

In Jesus' name,
Amen

April 12

"For I the LORD do not change."
Malachi 3:6

My Prayer

Dear Heavenly Father,

Oh, how I love knowing You do not change, Lord! Your character remains the same— always. You tell the mountains to move and they move. You make things happen for good for those who love You. I believe all things are working out for good. I have found joy even in the struggles. I am stronger knowing that Your promises are true and constant. You never change the genuine love You have for me. Thank You for being ever-present in my life! I am free in You! I love You, Lord!

In Jesus' name,
Amen

April 13

"As each has received a gift, use it to serve one another, as good stewards of God's varied grace."
1 Peter 4:10

My Prayer

Dear Heavenly Father,

Oh, how I thank You for giving me gifts I can use to help others grow in faith. You have put people in my life who have strengthened mine. May I continue honoring You by reaching out to others with these special gifts You have given me. We all need You, Lord! We all need to grow our faith especially in the days ahead. Increase our faith, Lord! We will grow in grace and love together when we let You work in us and through us as Your hands and feet ready to serve!

In Jesus' name,
Amen

April 14

"You have kept count of my tossings; put my tears in you bottle. Are they not in your book?"
Psalm 56:8

My Prayer

Dear Heavenly Father,

You are my Comforter and my Healer. Thank You for helping me in my times of need. As I weep, You collect my tears and hold me tight. I can feel Your hand comforting me as I go through challenges and trials. I can hear Your soothing voice helping me. As I surrender my worries, You give me greater hope. In Your presence there is fullness of joy! I will cling to You even more in these times, my Lord, as You hold me tight and keep me safe in Your arms!

In Jesus' name,
Amen

April 15

"My grace is sufficient for you, for my power is made perfect in weakness."
2 Corinthians 12:9

My Prayer

Dear Heavenly Father,

Thank You for giving me grace upon grace. In my weakest times, You are my strength. When I am anxious and overwhelmed, You pour Your love and grace over me. When I feel like I cannot go another step, all I need to do is call out Your name and You are there for me. You are a very present help in trouble! My Lord, thank You for rescuing me! I am redeemed and restored by Your amazing grace over me!

In Jesus' name,
Amen

April 16

"Why are you so afraid? Have you still no faith?"
Mark 4:40

My Prayer

Dear Heavenly Father,

You are so faithful, Lord! Help me to remain faithful to You without letting fear take over. I know there are days when I will be tempted to doubt. But You say run to You with even more faith, and I will, Lord. Thank You for helping me to see You with fresh eyes of faith each day. I will remain strong and courageous as I stay close to You. I will renew my strength in the challenge as I stretch my faith even more. Even in this struggle, I will look to faith and find the joy that is mine as Your child!

In Jesus' name,
Amen

April 17

"Oh, taste and see that the Lord is good!
Blessed is the man who takes refuge in Him!"
Psalm 34:8

My Prayer

Dear Heavenly Father,

My Lord, You are so wonderful! You bring me so much joy and love as I bask with awe and wonder in Your presence. I am alive with hope as I reflect on all Your incredible blessings of joy. These blessings that continue to grow as I trust You more and more. I am so thankful as I cling to Your promises and see Your unwavering character. I am full of joy as I rest in Your refuge, and I bask in Your grace that You have lavished upon me. I am renewed and have tasted, and I have seen that You are so good!

In Jesus' name,
Amen

April 18

"The LORD has established his throne in the heavens, and His kingdom rules over all."
Psalm 103:19

My Prayer

Dear Heavenly Father,

I am so very thankful for You, my Lord! Your love rules in my heart because I have made You my Lord and Savior. Your kingdom reigns in the heavens and on earth. You are in all and over all. I am grateful for Your abundant blessings over all of us. Help us to see and hear You with new eyes and ears of faith today and every day going forward. As we pray, restore Your Spirit within us. Create in us a new heart to love others as You love us. Seal us with Your Holy Spirit as we surrender all to You!

In Jesus' name,
Amen

April 19

"Peace I leave with you; my peace I give to you. Not as the world gives do I give to you. Let your hearts not be troubled, neither let them be afraid."
John 14:27

My Prayer

Dear Heavenly Father,

Thank You for Your perfect peace that remains forever. I am praising You for Your peace that dwells within me. As I seek more of You, I will find more of Your peace. This I know and believe: *More of You brings more peace*. I am seeking more of You today, my Lord. You provide all that I need as I rest in You. Lead me in the way of everlasting peace in Your presence!

In Jesus' name,
Amen

April 20

His Promise

"I will give them a heart to know that I am the LORD,
and they shall be my people and I will be their God,
for they shall return to me with their whole heart."
Jeremiah 24:7

My Prayer

Dear Heavenly Father,

Oh, how I thank You for being my Lord! I have
returned to You with my whole heart. I can rest
knowing You have everything planned for me. As I
follow You and let You show me the way I should go,
I will not fret, but will pray even more faithfully! You
tell me to trust You with all my heart and lean not on
my own understanding. I will lean on You every day,
in every way, my Lord and Savior! I am renewed and
restored in Your presence, my Lord!

In Jesus' name,
Amen

April 21

"But put on the Lord Jesus Christ, and make no provision for the flesh, to gratify its desires."
Romans 13:14

My Prayer

Dear Heavenly Father,

You give me hope, Lord, as I live and love with Your Spirit in me! I will put You on as I let You guide and direct me in all that I do. I can walk away from temptation as I lean on You, Lord. You are my strength! You give me life and peace as I trust You with all my heart. I am Your child, full of hope and joy in my heart instead of fear and anxiety. I will cling to Your promises and believe You will do what You say You will do! You are always faithful! I love You!

In Jesus' name,
Amen

April 22

His Promise

"You who have made me see many troubles and calamities will revive me again; from the depths of the earth you will bring me up again."
Psalm 71:20

My Prayer

Dear Heavenly Father,

I know You are working in my life to revive me again and again. When I am weak, You are strong. When I am restless and full of anxiety, You give me perfect peace. What do I need? You know what I need even before I ask. I am crying out to You for help. I need revival! I need healing in every part of me— physically, spiritually, and mentally. Thank You for hearing my prayers and responding to me. I need You, Lord. Your love, grace, and power have awakened me!

In Jesus' name,
Amen

April 23

His Promise

"Be exalted O God, above the heavens!
Let your glory be over all the earth!"
Psalm 108:5

My Prayer

Dear Heavenly Father,

I exalt You, Lord! You reign above all and are in all! As I ponder Your many blessings upon me, I am encouraged, full of praise, and thankful. I lift my prayers to You, Lord. I see the wonder and awe and am inspired by Your love for me. Help me to see what is possible with You and not focus on what seems impossible. All things are possible with You, my Lord! Great is Your faithfulness!

In Jesus name,
Amen

April 24

"For freedom Christ has set us free; stand firm, therefore, and do not submit again to a yoke of slavery."
Galatians 5:1

My Prayer

Dear Heavenly Father,

Thank You, Lord, for setting me free! As I reflect on this truth today, I am filled with hope. It is for freedom, that You have set me free, and I am alive and full of joy! I am so humbled and thankful for this promise of freedom that is mine in You. This promise from You is real and I will not take it for granted. When I think of how much grace You give me and how much You love me, I am living in that freedom again and again. It is for freedom that You live in me and have set me free! Hallelujah, I am alive!

In Jesus' name,
Amen

April 25

His Promise

*"The Lord is not slow to fulfill His promise as some
count slowness, but is patient toward you, not wishing
that any should perish, but that all should reach
repentance."*
2 Peter 3:9

My Prayer

Dear Heavenly Father,

Thank You for giving me the gift of Your presence.
In You, I am alive and free! You give me hope when
I rest in You. I hear You calling me closer to Your
love and I am encouraged. Give me eyes to see You
and ears to hear You as I wait patiently
for You, my Lord! I am so thankful
for You. I will continue trusting
and praying knowing You will
answer me in Your perfect
timing! I believe without
fully seeing because I have
mountain-moving faith that
grows stronger as I wait for
You. I love You with all my
heart!

In Jesus' name,
Amen

April 26

"Behold, God is my helper;
the LORD is the upholder of my life."
Psalm 54:4

My Prayer

Dear Heavenly Father,

You are my Helper, Lord! I know You will watch out for me and help me as I draw closer to You. Even in the hard times, You are close. All I need to do is call out to You and You will be a very present help in trouble. I am pressing into Your promises and will remain faithful to You. Thank You for giving me renewed hope! I am clinging tightly to You and am comforted by Your presence and faithfulness. You are the upholder of my life!

In Jesus' name,
Amen

April 27

"Finally, be strong in the Lord and in the strength of his might."
Ephesians 6:10

My Prayer

Dear Heavenly Father,

I will be strong in Your might and power, Lord! You are calling me to come closer and not be afraid. I hear Your soothing voice giving me courage and strength for whatever challenges are before me. I will live in the Spirit with You where there is life and peace, and I will walk with hope once again. There is no need to worry when You are near! You are calling me to come closer to see the miracles! I can see, Lord, as I pray, all the amazing miracles You have been waiting to show me!

In Jesus' name,
Amen

April 28

"God is our refuge and strength;
a very present help in trouble."
Psalm 46:1

My Prayer

Dear Heavenly Father,

I know You are always there for me.
When I need help, You are near and
will be a refuge for me. All I need to
do is come closer to You, my Lord.
Thank You for giving me hope once
again. I can rest knowing that You
will always be there for me. As I
await answers to my prayers, I am
strengthened by Your abundant grace and
steadfast love. I feel Your perfect peace
and I rest in Your presence. There is
fullness of joy where You are, my Lord!
Thank You for being my refuge! I love
You!

In Jesus' name,
Amen

April 29

*"I wait for the LORD, my soul waits,
and in his word I hope."*
Psalm 130:5

My Prayer

Dear Heavenly Father,

Oh, how long must I wait, my Lord? I know Your answers will come. As I wait, I will worship You even more. I have hope in Your promises and trust You to do what You say. There are prayers I have been praying so long now but I know they will be answered in Your timing. I will wait and be still before You. In Your presence, there is fullness of great joy. I wait because I can feel Your strength and power working inside me. I know all things will work out for good for all who love You and I do love You!

In Jesus' name,
Amen

April 30

"For we walk by faith, not by sight."
2 Corinthians 5:7

My Prayer

Dear Heavenly Father,

Thank You for always being there beside me to guide me. Even when I cannot see, I know You are with me. I will keep walking by faith and not by sight and abiding in Your love more and more. You have promised to be with me always, even in the valleys and on the mountains, and this encourages me so much. I can do all things through You who strengthens me! I am hopeful for what is to come and so very thankful for Your many blessings!

In Jesus' name,
Amen

For I know the plans I have for you, declares the Lord, plans for welfare and not for evil, to give you a future and a hope.

JEREMIAH 29:11

May 1

"Be still and know that I am God."
Psalm 46:10

My Prayer

Dear Heavenly Father,

I know You are near, Lord, when I am still and quiet before You. You are protecting me and helping me. I believe Your promises You have given me. I wait upon You. I will continue being still before You, my Lord. Help me keep close with eyes of faith. When I listen, I can hear You in the stillness of my soul. I can see You when I look up. Thank You for bending down to listen to me as I pray. I will keep abiding in You and praying faithfully as I remain in You and You in me.

In Jesus' name,
Amen

May 2

"And when Jesus saw their faith, he said to the paralytic, 'Son your sins are forgiven.'"
Mark 2:5

My Prayer

Dear Heavenly Father,

I know You hear my prayers of faith. I am praying for people on my heart who need You and Your healing. I believe You will heal them. I am not doubting but am continuing to believe that You will heal them physically, spiritually, and mentally. Only You, my Lord, can bring the needed restoration. You promise to help us when we lean in closer and call upon You. You give us hope when we trust You to provide all that we need. I am grateful for Your promises, Lord. I am strong in my faith when I keep holding on faithfully to You. Hear my prayers for healing!

In Jesus' name,
Amen

May 3

*"So I have looked upon you in the sanctuary,
beholding your power and glory."*
Psalm 63:2

My Prayer

Dear Heavenly Father,

I adore You, O Lord! As I gaze upon You in the
sanctuary, I feel Your power and glory upon me. I see
the light of Your love shining on me and I am so
overwhelmed with joy! The peace You give me is
like no other. As I am still in Your presence, I feel the
warmth of the light of Your love, and it soothes my
soul. I hear Your gentle whispers of hope and feel
certain that You will help me. I will keep my gaze
upon You, my Lord and Savior, and will rejoice in
Your majesty and glory forever and ever!

In Jesus' name,
Amen

May 4

His Promise

"The LORD will fight for you,
and you have only to be silent."
Exodus 14:14

My Prayer

Dear Heavenly Father,

Thank You for fighting my battles! I know that if I pray and let You take control, You will fight for me. I have been trying to face everything alone without You. I am stronger in Your presence because I press on with Your help. For You are all powerful and mighty, Lord. With You, I can face anything! I will be silent and let You fight for me. I am blessed to have Your power taking over the battle for me. I will press on toward victory and let You fight for me!

In Jesus' name,
Amen

May 5

*"I waited patiently for the LORD; he inclined to me
and heard my cry."*
Psalm 40:1

My Prayer

Dear Heavenly Father,

Thank You for Your patience and understanding with
me. I, in return, will be patient as I am waiting for
answers. I will trust Your timing and stop doubting.
You have the perfect plan and know when things will
work out. You ask me to trust and obey even without
knowing all the details. I know my faith will grow
while I wait, even as I struggle. Your testing has
come, and I want to remain faithful to You. Not all
have faith, but You are faithful and able to do
anything! I will pray for all to come repentance so
You will save and heal us! I do believe as I patiently
wait and fervently pray.

In Jesus' name,
Amen

May 6

His Promise

For to set the mind on flesh is death, but to set the mind on the Spirit is life and peace."
Romans 8:6

My Prayer

Dear Heavenly Father,

Thank You for giving me new life and peace as I set my mind on You. I will not be conformed to the world and its mindset but will be transformed by You. I will let You lead me into all truth. It is so wonderful to be in Your presence, Lord! I am spiritually full when I stay close to You. I will keep believing Your promises to me and trusting You each step of the way. There is a way with the Spirit close to me. In Your presence there is fullness of joy and complete peace! I am empowered to new life in You, Lord Jesus!

In Jesus' name,
Amen

May 7

His Promise

"Ask, and it will be given to you; seek and you will find; knock and the door will be opened to you."
Matthew 7:7

My Prayer

Dear Heavenly Father,

I begin this day by asking boldly for what is on my heart. I am seeking You with my whole heart. I am eager to see how You will open the door when I seek more of You and walk by faith. I know Your answers will come in Your perfect timing as I surrender and let You show me the way. I do not need to worry or doubt, but trust You, my Lord, to always be faithful. Open the door that no man can shut!

In Jesus' name,
Amen

May 8

*"So faith comes from hearing,
and hearing through the word of Christ."*
Romans 10:17

My Prayer

Dear Heavenly Father,

I know You want me to have more faith. I will listen so that I can hear Your words to me. My faith is growing stronger as I lean in closer to You. I will keep my eyes upon You as I walk obediently with Your hand upon me. You are always with me, and I am relying upon You to save and deliver me! Thank You for Your promises that I can stand upon with assurance and hope. You are so faithful, and I am blessed, indeed! I do hear You!

In Jesus' name,
Amen

May 9

<u>His Promise</u>

"If you abide in my word, you are truly my disciples, and you will know the truth, and the truth will set you free."
John 8:31-32

<u>My Prayer</u>

Dear Heavenly Father,

The truth has set me free! I know You and Your promises and I am relying on You with utmost faith. I believe what You have said to be true as I worship and praise You. I will direct my heart to Your voice and listen to what You say. You have spoken truth to me, so I will lean on Your promises and not on my own understanding. As I abide in You, my faith will grow exponentially! Thank You for pouring Your love over me and blessing me with peace and freedom!

In Jesus' name,
Amen

May 10

"Come to me, all who labor and are heavy laden, and I will give you rest."
Matthew 11:28

My Prayer

Dear Heavenly Father,

Thank You for giving me rest, my Lord. I am praying for refuge and strength. I know You are my very present help when I am tired and weary. I will let go of my worry and let you give me rest. These burdens I have are opportunities to pray and to trust. As I lift up my concerns to You I already feel better. In Your presence, with Your hand upon me, I am content and full of peace!

In Jesus' name,
Amen

May 11

"For he who is in you is greater than he who is in the world."
1 John 4:4

My Prayer

Dear Heavenly Father,

I am praising You today for Your greatness and majesty over all. You have the final say over what will be because Your glory reigns forever! I am thankful for Your countless blessings of peace over me as I trust You with all my heart. I will not lean on the world but will lean on You more and more. It is comforting and good to be close to You, my Lord. Your presence overpowers and overwhelms me day by day. Thank You for being my all in all! I love You!

In Jesus' name,
Amen

May 12

"On the day I called, you answered me;
my strength of soul you increased."
Psalm 138:3

My Prayer

Dear Heavenly Father,

In my weakness, You will be my strength! I need You, my Lord, to help me! I am searching for refuge from this storm. Only You can save and strengthen me! Help me to reach out to You even when I cannot see what I know You have promised me. I will walk by faith and not by sight. I will press on with positivity even in struggle. I will trust and obey as I pray for direction. I will go as You have called me…one faithful step at a time!

In Jesus' name,
Amen

May 13

*"I wait for the LORD, my soul waits,
and in his word I hope."*
Psalm 130:5

My Prayer

Dear Heavenly Father,

I will wait for You, my Lord. My soul is yearning for more of You, so I will be still before You. In the waiting, You will show me the way. In the seeking, I will find. In the stillness of my soul, I will be enriched and renewed by You. And as I pray today, I will be patient and hopeful for the things to come. Only You can mend my broken heart. Only You can save me. Only You can restore me. I will wait patiently upon You as I pray and believe Your promises to me!

In Jesus' name,
Amen

May 14

"Why are you afraid, O you of little faith?"
Matthew 8:26

My Prayer

Dear Heavenly Father,

Help my unbelief and increase my faith, Lord! I need to stretch my faith when I wake up today to a new day of opportunities to grow. Let my actions be proof of my growing faith. I will keep praying in faith for what You have promised me. I will touch the healing for myself and others as I touch You. Your healing touch has opened my heart to believe! Nothing is too hard for You, my Lord! I do believe!

In Jesus' name,
Amen

May 15

His Promise

"For by grace you have been saved through faith. And this is not your own doing; it is the gift of God."
Ephesians 2:8

My Prayer

Dear Heavenly Father,

I want to be set free! I will keep trusting You so that I can be free indeed! You are my Lord and Savior full of love and grace. I am most thankful for Your ever-present grace for me! Help me to let go and let You show me the way. In Your presence, I can escape my problems and rest in You. I will keep close so You can rescue me. I will surrender all and let You restore me. You are my forever friend! I love You!

In Jesus' name,
Amen

May 16

His Promise

"And he said to the woman, "Your faith has saved you; go in peace."
Luke 7:50

My Prayer

Dear Heavenly Father,

I want to have mountain-moving faith! As I do, You will give me renewed peace. I will trust You as You desire and let You fill me with faith. This faith will bring much needed peace into my heart. I am so full of hope as I enter this place of peace with You. I can rest and feel Your heartbeat. I hear You speak love to me, and Your eternal joy enters my soul. It is well with me!

In Jesus' name,
Amen

May 17

"I came that they may have life and have it abundantly."
John 10:10

My Prayer

Dear Heavenly Father,

Thank You for giving me life! You have promised abundant life to me, and I am hopeful and joyful for this life in You! You will touch me when I ask for healing. You will encourage me when I ask for help. You will show me the way when I ask for direction. You have touched me with Your love. The Spirit has come alive in me, and I surrender to you, Lord, and will let you touch my heart again. Thank You for these touches and for the abundant life that is in You!

In Jesus' name,
Amen

May 18

His Promise

*"And behold, I am with you always,
to the end of the age."*
Matthew 28:20

My Prayer

Dear Heavenly Father,

I have hope because I have a relationship with You. I know You are with me always because that is Your promise to me. I am hopeful because of the truth you have spoken to me, and I am relying on Your promises to me. Thank You for giving me security as I come closer to You. Thank You for Your goodness and mercy that never ends. Great is Your faithfulness to me! I am basking in Your presence as I see Your glory all around me!

In Jesus' name,
Amen

May 19

*"But I say, walk by the Spirit, and you will not gratify
the desires of the flesh."*
Galatians 5:16

My Prayer

Dear Heavenly Father,

I know You want me to walk by the Spirit. You tell
me that when I do, I will be living the way that leads
to life. The Spirit will help me when I need direction.
The Spirit will teach me when I need guidance. The
Spirit will touch me when I need comforting. The
Spirit will restore me when I need hope. The Spirit
will bring me all that I need! I will walk by the Spirit
more and more to see You working and awakened in
me, Lord!

In Jesus' name,
Amen

May 20

*"Fear not, for I have redeemed you; I have called you
by name, you are mine."*
Isaiah 43:1

My Prayer

Dear Heavenly Father,

I will not be afraid because I have You with me. You
have redeemed me and called me by name. I am
Yours, Lord, ready to step out without fear and with
Your courage and strength. Help me to lean closer on
You and be encouraged in the days ahead. I am
challenged but not broken. I am tired but will not give
up. I hear You calling my name. I am ready to go
where You lead me with Your Spirit alive inside me
and guiding me. Thank You for loving me with Your
steadfast love so I can be fearless and free!

In Jesus' name,
Amen

May 21

His Promise

"So now faith, hope, and love abide, these three; but the greatest of these is love."
1 Corinthians 13:13

My Prayer

Dear Heavenly Father,

Thank You for loving me! With love, You bend down to listen as I pray. I am basking in the beauty of Your love, and I find peace in Your presence. Help me to love others as You love me. Give me the will to forgive as You have forgiven me. Grant me strength to press on with joy as I come closer to Your love. I believe what You have promised me. I will press on to the prize of the upward call of Jesus Christ who gives me the greatest gift— Unconditional love!

In Jesus' name,
Amen

May 22

"All things are possible for one who believes."
Mark 9:23

My Prayer

Dear Heavenly Father,

Help my unbelief, Lord! You are so faithful and have told me that everything is possible for the one who believes! I will keep praying big knowing that the miracle is coming for me. I will hold on to what You have promised me. The healing is possible if it be Your will. I am praying for healing and wholeness where there is sickness and brokenness. I know You can do what is impossible for man. I will keep trusting You with all my heart and lean not on my own understanding. In all my ways I will acknowledge You so that You can make my path straight. I do believe!

In Jesus' name,
Amen

May 23

"If you will walk in my statutes and obey my rules and keep all my commandments and walk in them, then I will establish my word with you."
1 Kings 6:12

My Prayer

Dear Heavenly Father,

You want me to obey You by keeping Your commandments and walking in them. I know the right way to go as I read Your Word and listen to Your voice. Thank You for giving me the Holy Spirit who guides me to all truth. I will walk in the Spirit who brings life-giving power. Thank You for speaking truth to me. I hear You and will obey as I draw closer in prayer. Thank You for bending Your ear to me as I pray for guidance and strength. I cherish Your love and will follow You all the days of my life!

In Jesus' name,
Amen

May 24

His Promise

"Behold, God is my helper;
the Lord is the upholder of my life."
Psalm 54:4

My Prayer

Dear Heavenly Father,

You are my Helper, Lord. I come to You with burdens today that I need to release to You. Thank You for attending to the voice of my prayers. I am weary and need greater faith. My unbelief creeps up when I see the problems before me. But You, O God, will rescue me when I release control over to You. Thank you for holding me up! I am steady and stronger with You as my anchor. I will keep praying and will believe in what You have promised me!

In Jesus' name,
Amen

May 25

"I praise you, for I am fearfully and wonderfully made. Wonderful are your works; my soul knows it very well."
Psalm 139:14

My Prayer

Dear Heavenly Father,

I am basking in Your glory and praising You for Your wonderful works! How peaceful it is to sit in Your presence! How amazing it is to see all You have created! I am praising You for putting hope in my heart when I gaze upon Your majesty time and time again. From the sun rising to its setting, You are there for me! I am not alone when I remember how much You love me. I am fearfully and wonderfully made in Your image out of love. Thank You for showing me You love me! I love You with all my heart, my Lord, my constant companion.

In Jesus' name,
Amen

May 26

"And blessed is she who believed that there would be a fulfillment of what was spoken to her from the Lord."
Luke 1:45

My Prayer

Dear Heavenly Father,

You always keep your promises. You tell us that if we are faithful and obedient, we will see Your promises come to life. I believe in the words you speak to me. What You say is truth. I will not waver in my faith because You are faithful. I am relying on You, my Lord. Your power has given me new strength to press on in all circumstances. Your bountiful blessings have come to my life, and I am blessed with utmost joy deep in my heart!

In Jesus' name,
Amen

May 27

"They may be called oaks of righteousness, the planting of the LORD that he might be glorified.
Isaiah 61:3

My Prayer

Dear Heavenly Father,

You have made Your people out of love with hearts to praise and worship You. Each person is crafted with love by You so they can be saved by grace and filled with Your righteousness. Help us all to look up to You and praise You no matter what we are facing. You will give us strength and power as we press on obediently with our actions of faith. Let us not stop hoping and praying for what You have promised us! It is by faith, through grace, that we are saved! We will stand tall like oaks of righteousness as we stand on Your Promises!

In Jesus' name,
Amen

May 28

"For our God is a consuming fire."
Hebrews 12:29

My Prayer

Dear Heavenly Father,

Thank You for loving me. I will worship You and am so thankful for Your magnificent power and glory over me. I have been praying for Your perfect peace to rest over me. And as I worship You in reverence and awe, You give me strength to press on. As I surrender, I see more of Your holiness surround me. Help me to rest knowing You have my whole life in Your hands. You have consumed my life with joy and Your fire is burning brightly within me!

In Jesus' name,
Amen

May 29

*"Do not be anxious about anything, but in everything
by prayer and supplication with thanksgiving let your
requests be made known to God."*
Philippians 4:6

My Prayer

Dear Heavenly Father,

Oh, how I love You, Lord! You have promised to
help me overcome my anxiety and worry. I will trust
You even more, right now, knowing You will help
me with what I am facing. Even in this uncertainty,
You keep telling me to press on to the promise and
keep believing in the miracle. I do believe and will
keep praying and trusting You in all circumstances.
You are so faithful! I need
You, Lord!

In Jesus' name,
Amen

May 30

"My soul waits for the Lord more than watchmen for the morning, more than watchmen for the morning."
Psalm 130:6

My Prayer

Dear Heavenly Father,

I will wait patiently upon You, my Lord, and I will trust You. I believe as sure as the sun rises that You will help me rise above all problems and challenges. You know what I am facing at each moment and promise to help me when I keep my faith, confidence, and trust in You. I will not be afraid but will trust You to do what You say. I cannot wait to see the miracles come to life! I have this hope that only comes from You, and I cherish it deep in my soul. I am hopeful for what I cannot see and I believe as I keep lifting my prayers to You!

In Jesus' name,
Amen

May 31

"Great are the works of the LORD, studied by all who delight in them."
Psalm 111:2

My Prayer

Dear Heavenly Father,

Thank You for your wonderful works of love all around me. I am praising You for creating me in Your image out of love. I am thankful for all You are doing in me. My heart knows Your love very well and I am basking in the glory of Your love deep down in my soul. As I reach up to You, You keeping reminding me who is in control. I am grateful for Your faithfulness and for Your blessings of everlasting love shining down brightly on me!

In Jesus' name,
Amen

"The Lord is my portion,"
says my soul, therefore,
I hope in him."

LAMENTATIONS 3:24

June 1

*"So I will bless you as long as I live;
in your name I will lift up my hands."*
Psalm 63:4

My Prayer

Dear Heavenly Father,

Thank You for all You are and what You are doing in my life. You give me hope when I praise You. I am fearless with praise as I trust You in all circumstances to help me. I am leaning upon Your promises and praising You for every one of them! I am sure about what You have promised me and am listening to what You say. I will act and walk by faith and not by my sight, my Lord, but Yours. You see all and are in all and I am praising You while I put my faith first!

In Jesus' name,
Amen

June 2

His Promise

"Rejoice in the Lord always;
again I will say, rejoice."
Philippians 4:4

My Prayer

Dear Heavenly Father,

I will rejoice with You today my, Lord! You are so wonderful to give me another day to praise You for Your glorious blessings! Your love is so amazing! I feel Your love envelope every part of my body and light up my soul as the sun rises over me. As I share Your love with those around me, I receive even more of Your love. I give You honor and praise for giving me a new day to share Your love. I am rejoicing because I am renewed each day! I love You with my whole heart! Thank You for loving me!

In Jesus' name,
Amen

June 3

*"Humble yourselves before the Lord,
and He will exalt you."*
James 4:10

My Prayer

Dear Heavenly Father,

I come to You humbly and earnestly in prayer. I thank You for helping me. As I look with eyes of faith, I am thankful to see what You want me to see. I hear You calling my name when I pray. You promise to help me as I seek You. I am grateful for Your constant companionship. You never leave me. I love being in Your presence, Lord, where there is peace. As I look to You, I find all that I need! I am praising You, Lord, for You are my all in all!

In Jesus' name,
Amen

June 4

"Draw near to God, and he will draw near to you."
James 4:8

My Prayer

Dear Heavenly Father,

I will wait upon You and believe in Your promises to me. You have brought me so much hope in the waiting as I draw near to You! I do see what You want to show me, and I'm certain of what You want me to do. You want me to trust You with all my heart. You desire that I obey You even when I do not understand. You are calling me to step out of my comfort zone and believe Your promises to me with all my soul so that You can show me the way that is best for me. I will trust and I will obey You as I boldly live out my faith one step at a time!

In Jesus' name,
Amen

June 5

"You are a hiding place for me; you preserve me from trouble; you surround me with shouts of deliverance."
Psalm 32:7

My Prayer

Dear Heavenly Father,

You are my hiding place, Lord, a refuge from the storms! All is well with my soul in Your presence. You have brought me to a place where I can be still and find rest. I am comforted in Your sweet embrace. I am at peace with You near me. I am praying for a new spark of hope to rise above any fear. As my faith grows, You help me see the promise of refuge and rest that is mine in You. My worries disappear when I draw closer to You! I am free and full of Your perfect peace as You have delivered me!

In Jesus' name,
Amen

June 6

His Promise

"Christ is all, and in all."
Colossians 3:11

My Prayer

Dear Heavenly Father,

I have such hope because You are ever-present. Thank You for helping me see You in all I do! I will let go and let You lead me. I trust and obey. You are everything to me! Your presence gives me hope and peace. I am thankful for the blessings of Your love and grace. I will be calm and at peace as I lift my heart to You in praise and thanksgiving for Your steadfast promises. I am standing on Your faithful promises, my Lord, my all in all!

In Jesus' name,
Amen

June 7

"Stretch out your hand."
Mark 3:5

My Prayer

Dear Heavenly Father,

I know that if I stretch my hands to You in faith that You will help me. You will heal me. I will keep stretching my faith even when I cannot see all the details. I am grateful for Your healing presence in me. I am walking by faith with my eyes wide open to see You at work around me. I will join You in what you need me to do one day at a time. I will take Your hand, my Lord, and live out my faith. Here is my hand, Lord, I believe!

In Jesus' name,
Amen

June 8

"For your steadfast love is before my eyes,
and I walk in your faithfulness."
Psalm 26:3

My Prayer

Dear Heavenly Father,

Your steadfast love has set me apart to love others. I am walking by faith, and I trust You more each day. You have called me to extend love to others. Work in me so that I can serve You and be all that You need be to be. Your love is better than life! I am praying for endurance so I may press on faithfully with Your steadfast love and power strengthening me for any challenge. I hear Your gentle voice of encouragement leading me to greater faith. I am stronger when I am closer to You, my Lord!

In Jesus' name,
Amen

June 9

His Promise

"They who wait for the LORD shall renew their strength; they shall mount up with wings like eagles; they shall run and not be weary; they shall walk and not faint."
Isaiah 40:31

My Prayer

Dear Heavenly Father,

Thank You for giving me strength as I wait for You with hope. I am weary from all that I have before me. But I know You will infuse me when I run to You. I am thankful I can rely upon You, my Lord! No matter what I face, You are there for me. I can see Your hand upon me helping me one step at a time. In these days ahead, I will be empowered to run and not lose faith. I can get up and walk with confidence and not faint. I am close to You, and I look forward to these days You have given me, O my Lord, the Keeper of my heart and Strengthener of my soul!

In Jesus' name,
Amen

June 10

His Promise

"So then, brothers, stand firm and hold to the traditions that you were taught by us, either by our spoken word or by our letter."
2 Thessalonians 2:15

My Prayer

Dear Heavenly Father,

Help me to stand firm and hold to the traditions that You taught me, O Lord! I will not waver in my belief. My faith is getting stronger as I trust You even more. I am eager to see what You will do as I continue growing in the faith day by day. I know You give me hope to believe when I keep loving You. There is nothing that is impossible for You as I keep trusting You. Nothing is too hard for You! I will deepen my faith and listen as You speak truth to me. I will stand firm and believe!

In Jesus' name,
Amen

June 11

His Promise

"You have put more joy in my heart..."
Psalm 4:7

My Prayer

Dear Heavenly Father,

I am full of joy with You in my heart! I am floating with so much joy from Your love that has come to life in me! As I wait for You to answer the deepest desires of my heart, I have complete joy that I cannot explain. In the waiting, my faith is growing. In the searching, I surrender fully to You. I feel Your overwhelming presence connecting me to the joy You want to give me. I need You, my Lord, always and forever in my heart. I am devoted to You and will look to You for all that I need. I love You so very much, my Lord, my Joy!

In Jesus' name,
Amen

June 12

"He himself is our peace."
Ephesians 2:14

My Prayer

Dear Heavenly Father,

I know You are my peace. Thank You for covering me with this peace even in all my most difficult and disappointing circumstances. I hear You telling me to be still and feel Your peace over me. I will let go of my burdens and let Your peace permeate every part of me. As I rest in You, I feel safe and secure. Nothing can come between You and me. Your love remains in me, and Your peace is real. You are my peace, my Lord, present in and around me!

In Jesus' name,
Amen

June 13

*"Blessed is he whose help is the God of Jacob,
whose hope is in the LORD his God."*
Psalm 146:5

My Prayer

Dear Heavenly Father,

I have my steadfast hope placed in You, my Lord! There is nothing impossible for You! Thank You for helping me whenever I need You. I can turn to You for comfort and refuge. I can lean on You for strength when I am weary. I can rest in Your presence in the struggle and feel peace that passes all understanding. I will not let go of You, my Lord! You are my strong tower and a very present help in trouble. My hope rests in You, now and forevermore!

In Jesus' name,
Amen

June 14

"Likewise, the Spirit helps us in our weakness, for we do not know what to pray for as we ought, but the Spirit himself intercedes for us with groaning too deep for words."
Romans 8:26

My Prayer

Dear Heavenly Father,

I need Your help, my Lord. There are days when I do not know what to pray and need the Holy Spirit to intercede for me. It is comforting to know You will be there for me any time I need You. You never leave me! It is so good to be able to ask You for what I need, knowing that You will help me! I am praying for restoration, revival, and renewal, my Lord. I am ready to see what You have in store for me so I may serve you. In Your presence there is fullness of great joy! In You, I have the strength I need!

In Jesus' name,
Amen

June 15

"Having the eyes of your hearts enlightened that you may know what is the hope to which he has called you, what are the riches of his glorious inheritance in the saints."
Ephesians 1:18

My Prayer

Dear Heavenly Father,

Thank You for giving me hope! My heart is full of the hope that comes from You! I am praying for my eyes to be enlightened with Your love as I draw closer to You in prayer. Thank You for putting Your Spirit in me so that I can see with spiritual eyes of faith. It is so good to see this way, my Lord! I can rise above my circumstances when I let Your Spirit come alive in me and allow my faith to grow. I will keep looking forward, believing Your promises of hope for me. Where the Spirit of the Lord is, there is freedom! I am following You to freedom!

In Jesus' name,
Amen

June 16

"He has made everything beautiful in its time. Also he has put eternity into man's heart, yet so that he cannot find out what God has done from the beginning to the end."
Ecclesiastes 3:11

My Prayer

Dear Heavenly Father,

I know Your timing is perfect! You will make everything beautiful in its time. Thank You for giving me hope as I pray remembering this promise. You make beauty out of ashes and bring light to the darkness. I have seen You do amazing things when Your people pray faithfully and patiently! You never forget the sweet praises and cries from the hearts lifted to You. As we pray, these prayers rise to You like incense with a sweet aroma. I will continue believing and praying with a patient hope rising inside me. Thank You, Lord, for making all things new and beautiful in Your perfect timing!

In Jesus' name,
Amen

June 17

"Behold, I have put my words in your mouth."
Jeremiah 1:9

My Prayer

Dear Heavenly Father,

Thank You for putting Your words in my mouth. I know You are ready for me to speak truth in love to strengthen and encourage others. You have given me so much love and grace to spread like salt and light to those around me. As I trust and obey, I will live with pure joy that only comes from You. This newfound joy is overflowing like rivers flowing from You and in and out of me. Your perfect peace is present in me as I bask in Your presence. I hear Your voice speaking to me as I listen carefully to obey You and prayerfully to trust You, my Lord!

In Jesus' name,
Amen

June 18

*"So teach us to number our days that we may get a
heart of wisdom."*
Psalm 90:12

My Prayer

Dear Heavenly Father,

I want to make the most of my time spent with You. I
will seek You with all my heart as I let You revive me
again! I need Your living water and daily bread to
work for Your glory! I know You will give me
wisdom as I seek guidance and counsel from Your
Word and the Holy Spirit within me. I am ready to
make a difference for You, my Lord! Show me the
places I can serve You and the ways
I can please You! I love You so
much, Lord! You have revived
me!

In Jesus' name,
Amen

June 19

"And I am sure of this, that he who began a good work in you will bring it to completion at the day of Jesus Christ."
Philippians 1:6

My Prayer

Dear Heavenly Father,

Give me strength to finish what you started! Help me to be faithful to the calling you have placed in my heart. As I listen to Your voice, I am sure of what You want me to do. Help me to be obedient so I may show my love for You! I am excited for what You have placed in front of me to do. And I am eager to see how things will work out for Your glory as I keep running my race with eyes fixed on You! I have the endurance I need from You as I press on with Your power and strength!

In Jesus' name,
Amen

June 20

"For you O LORD, have made me glad by your work;
at the works of your hands I sing for joy."
Psalm 92:4

My Prayer

Dear Heavenly Father,

O, how I long to see the works of Your hands all around me. I know You are working wonders among Your people. You are showing us great and mighty things if we would simply open our spiritual eyes to see! Thank You for showing me the joy all around me! In Your presence there is fullness of joy! At Your right hand are pleasures too great to count! I am basking in the goodness of who You are to me, today and every day! Thank You for always being there for me! I love You, Lord!

In Jesus' name,
Amen

June 21

*"For he himself is our peace, who has made us both
one and has broken down in his flesh the dividing
wall of hostility."*
Ephesians 2:14

My Prayer

Dear Heavenly Father,

You are my peace, Lord! I know the dividing wall of
hostility is present in this world, but You have
brought peace to all who will receive it, through Your
Son, Jesus Christ. Help us, Lord, to reach out in unity
instead of division. Let us show love to our neighbor
and pray for our enemies. In this world we will have
trouble, but You say to take heart, because You have
overcome the world with Your sacrifice of love! You
broke down the walls of hostility and division with
Your flesh so that we can live in peace and joy! I will
not listen to those who are hostile, but will hear Your
sweet voice lift me up where peace reigns! Thank
You for sacrificing Your life! I am free and alive in
You!

In Jesus' name,
Amen

June 22

,
"For when I am weak, then I am strong."
2 Corinthians 12:10

My Prayer

Dear Heavenly Father,

Thank You for strengthening me where I am weak. In my weakness, You infuse me with courage and vitality! In the challenges I face, You are there to encourage me. In the most difficult moments, You lift me up and my soul wakes up to new life with Your powerful presence. I will not let fear stop me from seeking You more. I will continue looking to You, the Author of my life! You have written my story and want me to keep the faith as I live it out. My destiny is in Your hands, O Lord! I will keep Your fire burning inside me! I am strong and stable in You!

In Jesus' name,
Amen

June 23

"Our God will fight for us."
Nehemiah 4:20

My Prayer

Dear Heavenly Father,

I surrender my whole heart to You, my Lord. Your love is so amazing! I am restored into good health spiritually, physically, and mentally when I stay close to You in the surrender. I know You have promised to fight all my battles. I will let You fight for me and stop stepping in like I have done before. All You ask of me is to seek You with my whole heart, be silent in the battle, and let You work all things out. You have promised to be my ever-present help in trouble. I will let go, surrender all, and let You fight for me, my Lord and Defender!

In Jesus' name,
Amen

June 24

"For it is God who works in you, both to will and to work for his good pleasure."
Philippians 2:13

My Prayer

Dear Heavenly Father,

Thank You for working in me! I know You have purposes in me that will be fulfilled as I draw closer to You. There are blessings waiting for those who love You and act according to Your will. I will be obedient and do what You ask so that I can witness Your work in and through me. There are abundant opportunities to shine the light of Your love. I will stay closely connected to You so I may be a part of the work You are doing around me— Work that is bringing people back to You. I am praising You for opening the eyes of my heart to see my purpose!

In Jesus' name,
Amen

June 25

"These things I have spoken to you, that my joy may be in you, and your joy may be full."
John 15:11

My Prayer

Dear Heavenly Father,

I will pause and lift my prayers to You, my Lord. Your presence is so uplifting to me. In the stillness of my soul, I feel Your love washing over me. In Your presence, there is fullness of great joy! I will listen to Your voice of encouragement when I pray. When I am still, I will open my heart to hear Your words of comfort and peace. I know that You are God and can do what seems impossible! I will keep believing for the miracles and keep hoping for what I do not yet see, centering my life on You and Your promises!

In Jesus' name,
Amen

June 26

"I have fought the good fight, I have finished the race, I have kept the faith."
2 Timothy 4:7

My Prayer

Dear Heavenly Father,

You want me to keep walking by faith. Even when things get tough, You promise to always be with me. I will turn faithfully to You so You can strengthen me in these challenges. You promise that I can do all things through You who strengthen me. I believe, and I am hopeful for what You have promised me. I am excited for what lies ahead as I walk victoriously by faith and not by sight. Thank You for helping me see the light! I will fight the good fight of the faith!

In Jesus' name,
Amen

June 27

His Promise

"The steadfast love of the LORD never ceases, his mercies never come to an end; they are new every morning;;great is your faithfulness."
Lamentations 3:22-23

My Prayer

Dear Heavenly Father,

Thank You for Your mercies that are new every morning! I need mercy and know that You will faithfully give me all that I need as I ask with a repentant heart. I am ready to experience all that You have prepared for me. I know You will help me as I ask and trust You more each day. As I do, my heart will be opened to receive more of Your enduring and steadfast love. How gracious You are to me, my Lord! You are my all in all!

In Jesus' name,
Amen

June 28

His Promise

"To you, O LORD, I lift up my soul.
O my God, in you I trust."
Psalm 25:1-2

My Prayer

Dear Heavenly Father,

I trust You, Lord! You know the best plans for me.
You know before I ask what I really need. I will keep
fervently praying. I bow down before You and
worship You, my Lord, for who You are! I know You
are able so I will keep looking up and believing! I
will give You my whole heart and put all my faith in
You. You are the one who will always be with me.
There is nowhere I can go that You will not be with
me. I will keep trusting You. I am no longer afraid,
but fearless and free with Your hand upon me!

In Jesus' name,
Amen

June 29

His Promise

"But truly God has listened;
he has attended to the voice of my prayer."
Psalm 66:19

My Prayer

Dear Heavenly Father,

Thank You for hearing me, O Lord, as I pray. You bend down to listen attentively to every single word I pray. How comforting to know I can talk to You anytime and You will be there for me. I do not have to wait to pray. You are there to listen and give me peace whenever I need You! I can be sure of Your love for me as I speak what is on my heart. You love it when I pray, and I love to talk with You. I will keep praying and praising You for creating me with the desire to pray and worship You, my Lord, my sweet Savior!

In Jesus' name,
Amen

June 30

"Yet even now, declares the LORD,
return to me with all your heart."
Joel 2:12

My Prayer

Dear Heavenly Father,

I know You want all people to return to You with whole hearts ready to be revived. You welcome us with open arms when we make the choice to come back. As we turn towards You, a fresh spark of revival will come to our heart and soul. May we all return to You, Lord, with our whole hearts to see the fires of revival burn brightly! We will see the revival we are praying for as we unite as one body and worship You in spirit and in truth! Hallelujah, Your love has reached, rescued, and revived us!

In Jesus' name,
Amen

Behold, the eye of the Lord is on those who fear him, on those who hope in his steadfast love.

PSALM 33:18

July 1

His Promise

"And I will give you a new heart, and a new spirit I will put within you. And I will remove the heart of stone from your flesh and give you a heart of flesh."
Ezekiel 36:26

My Prayer

Dear Heavenly Father,

Oh, how I long to hear Your voice, Lord. I will yield to You as I listen with my heart. Oh, how I yearn to see You, Lord. I will look to You with the eyes of my heart. Oh, how I need to touch You, Lord. I will open my arms to reach out and feel Your presence near me. I have Your Spirit alive and active within me when I listen, see, and touch You! Thank You for renewing me! I will worship You, O Lord, with a revived heart and spirit! It is well with my soul!

In Jesus' name,
Amen

July 2

*"The LORD is my light and my salvation; whom shall
I fear? The Lord is the stronghold of my life;
of whom shall I be afraid?"*
Psalm 27:1

My Prayer

Dear Heavenly Father,

I will not be afraid because You are near to me. You
are the stronghold of my life, and I will not let fear
creep up and stop me from wholeheartedly pursuing
You. I know You have promised to be with me as I
draw closer to Your light. Help me to walk by faith,
even in the hard times, instead of worrying about my
challenges. I am fearless because You are by my side!
Help me to run this race set before me with
determination, courage, and strength! I will run to
You, Lord, the Author of my life and Keeper of my
soul!

In Jesus' name,
Amen

July 3

His Promise

"Do not be overcome by evil,
but overcome evil with good."
Romans 12:21

My Prayer

Dear Heavenly Father,

You are always good, my Lord. Thank You for winning the victory over evil. I am so thankful that You came and conquered death. Nothing can stop Your powerful reign and presence! You are in all and over all! I feel You as I pour out my prayers. Your Spirit dwells securely in me so I can let good overshadow anything that tries to overcome me. You are so wonderful, my sweet Savior! Your love, goodness, and mercy always prevail, now and forevermore! I love You, Lord!

In Jesus' name,
Amen

July 4

"But as for me, I will look to the LORD; I will wait
for the God of my salvation; my God will hear me."
Micah 7:7

My Prayer

Dear Heavenly Father,

I know You hear me, Lord, as I pray to
You. You are waiting patiently for me
to lift my heart to You. The answers to
my questions will come when I lay
down my concerns and trust You to
work all things out. It is in the waiting
for answers that I am strengthened for
the challenges ahead of me. You have
infused me with spiritual power as I trust
You. You are a very present help in trouble when I
lift my petitions to You. Help my unbelief and renew
my faithfulness. I will look to You and believe, my
Lord, in this time of waiting! I trust You with all my
heart!

In Jesus' name,
Amen

July 5

*"Therefore since we are surrounded by so great a
cloud of witnesses, let us also lay aside every weight,
and sin which clings so closely, and let us run with
endurance the race that is set before us."*
Hebrews 12:1

My Prayer

Dear Heavenly Father,

I need perseverance to keep going. It is so easy to just
give up without Your constant companionship. But I
can run my race with endurance with You by my side.
Thank You for asking me to co-labor with You to
help build Your Kingdom. You need workers who
will not grow weary of doing Your will on earth. The
field is ready for harvest, and You have given me the
will to finish the work You began in me. I will throw
off the weight of sin from my past and set my eyes on
You, Lord Jesus! I am running this race set before me
with new hope because I have the living power of the
Holy Spirit alive in me! I am free, indeed!

In Jesus' name,
Amen

July 6

His Promise

*"Casting all your anxieties on him,
because he cares for you."*
1 Peter 5:7

My Prayer

Dear Heavenly Father,

I will give You all my cares and concerns because
You want to take them from me. You have peace for
me and want me to let go of worry and restlessness. I
will say goodbye to anxiety and hello to new peace
that will touch my soul. As I cast everything to You,
You will calm my anxious heart once again. I am
sorry that I keep taking back all those things that I
gave to You once before. I need to let go of control
once and for all. Lord, help me to be free from all that
is weighing me down! I praise You for Your rock of
refuge that brings me freedom and peace!

In Jesus' name,
Amen

July 7

*"For to set the mind on the flesh is death, but to set
the mind on the Spirit is life and peace."*
Romans 8:6

My Prayer

Dear Heavenly Father,

As I set my mind on the Spirit, I will find life and
peace. Even in the hardest of times, peace will rule in
me when I trust You. You promise a life of spiritual
blessings and strength when I live connected to the
Spirit. I will keep my mind on You, my Lord and
Redeemer, instead of on my problems. You are my
portion, now and forever. No one can separate me
from Your love! In Your presence, there is perfect
peace and fullness of life! I am praising You for these
promises of spiritual renewal!

In Jesus' name,
Amen

July 8

*"You have made known to me the paths of life; you
will make me full of gladness with your presence."*
Acts 2:28

My Prayer

Dear Heavenly Father,

I am full of gladness with Your presence in me. My
path of life is where You are, and I will follow You to
know a life full of joy that is waiting for me. I will not
fear when challenges come my way
but will trust You even more.
My faith will rise above any
fear or doubt. My attitude will
change from negative thoughts
to Your *positive promises.* In
the stillness of my soul is
where You are waiting for me.
I will be still and know that You are
God!

In Jesus' name,
Amen

July 9

"Arise, shine, for your light has come, and glory of the LORD has risen upon you."
Isaiah 60:1

My Prayer

Dear Heavenly Father,

Thank You for Your light! You have opened my eyes to see Your magnificent glory and I am alive with the power of Your Spirit in me! I will rise with You. I will let Your light of truth guide me. I am free as I walk in the light of Your love! I am praying for strength today as I keep in step with You. Thank You for shining Your light on me so that I can do all things through You who empower and strengthen me! I love You, Lord! Your glory reigns!

In Jesus' name,
Amen

July 10

"Count it all joy, my brothers, when you meet trials of various kinds, for you know that the testing of your faith produces steadfastness."
James 1:2-3

My Prayer

Dear Heavenly Father,

You will give me perseverance just when I need it, Lord! I am trusting You as I step out in faith even in the trials of life. I am stronger with Your mighty presence at work in me. Even when my faith is tested, I will persevere! You have promised to be near to those who trust You. I am holding on to You, Lord, and am confident that You will be with me as my trust and faith grow day by day. I believe in miracles, and I will claim Your miracle of new life and complete healing in Your presence, now and forevermore! I am healed!

In Jesus' name,
Amen

July 11

His Promise

"You keep him in perfect peace whose mind is stayed on you, because he trusts in you."
Isaiah 26:3

My Prayer

Dear Heavenly Father,

I will keep my mind on You to find peace. In Your presence there is perfect peace. Whenever I need more peace, I will look to You and trust You no matter what is going on around me. As I abide in You, peace flows through my soul and I hear Your soothing and comforting voice whispering love in my ear. I am encouraged to keep walking with Your peace reigning in me. I receive all that You want to give to me, my Lord, as I stay close to You and Your peace! I am alive with You in me!

In Jesus' name,
Amen

July 12

His Promise

"Behold, God is my salvation;
I will trust and will not be afraid for the LORD God
is my strength and my song, and he has become my
salvation."
Isaiah 12:2

My Prayer

Dear Heavenly Father,

I will trust You for courage because You promise to
be my strength. I will not be afraid but will let my
faith rise over any fear that may try to enter my
thoughts. As I trust You more and more, I feel hope
and peace even in times of trouble. You are my
refuge where I can be protected and secure. I do not
have to fear anymore because You have already won
the battle for me when You set me free from sin!
Thank You for being my salvation forevermore, so I
can keep going strong in the way of obedience and
courage!

In Jesus' name,
Amen

July 13

"Because I live, you also will live."
John 14:19

My Prayer

Dear Heavenly Father,

You are so amazing, Lord! Thank You for giving me new life. Because You live, I have life and peace flowing in me through Your living Spirit. I am at peace in Your presence and strong with Your power. Thank You for giving this new life to me when I first believed. Thank You for continuing to grow my faith as a child of the living God. I am renewed and restored because I have new life. Praise be to You, my God, for Your glory that reigns in all who believe! I am healed and made whole because You live in me!

In Jesus' name,
Amen

July 14

"So I have looked upon you in the sanctuary, beholding your power and glory. Because your steadfast love is better than life, my lips will praise you."
Psalm 63:2-3

My Prayer

Dear Heavenly Father,

I worship You and praise Your Holy name, my Lord! Each and every day I give thanks for your grace and love. Thank You for Your goodness and mercy that never ends! I will look to You for my strength. And, You my Lord, are my Strengthener of soul. Thank You for helping me one day at a time with Your hand upon me. Your mercies never end and are new every morning! Great is Your faithfulness! Your steadfast love is better than life!

In Jesus' name,
Amen

July 15

*"'Create in me a clean heart, O God,
and renew a right spirit within me."*
Psalm 51:10

My Prayer

Dear Heavenly Father,

Thank You for Your gift of grace. I ask for forgiveness for things that I have done that are not in Your will. Create in me a clean heart. Help renew a right spirit within me. I will honor You with my attitude of praise and thanksgiving. I repent of any negativity that has entered my thoughts. I will act out of love and forgiveness and know that my renewal of spirit will surely come as I draw closer to You. Praise and honor be to You, my Lord! I am restored and redeemed!

In Jesus' name,
Amen

July 16

"He who comes from above is above all. He who is of the earth belongs to the earth and speaks in an earthly way. He who comes from heaven is above all."
John 3:31

My Prayer

Dear Heavenly Father,

Your love is so amazing! You are above all and in all! Your power and might rise above all things. You are so wonderful and all You create is so beautiful. Your majesty brings wonder and awe to me! Thank You for Your never-ending goodness and mercy. Your steadfast love is powerful and reigns forever! I am basking in Your goodness and glory and will praise You all the days of my life!

In Jesus' name,
Amen

July 17

"Do not be afraid; you have done all this evil. Yet do not turn aside from following the LORD, but serve the Lord with all your heart."
1 Samuel 12:20

My Prayer

Dear Heavenly Father,

Yes, I will serve You with all my heart! I am dedicated to You and want to honor You with my service as You desire. You have given me a renewed passion to follow You as I keep trusting You with all my heart. You have turned my fear into joy and my disappointments to hope down deep in my soul. My doubts have dissipated as I serve You with a grateful heart. I love You, my Lord, and will commit my way to You!

In Jesus' name I pray,
Amen

July 18

His Promise

"Rise, and have no fear."
Matthew 17:7

My Prayer

Dear Heavenly Father,

I will rise and have no fear because You are near to me! My faith in You is rising over any fear that might try to creep up inside me. I can see what You promised me when I love with my heart wide open. I am renewed with spiritual strength as I stay connected to the Holy Spirit within me. I trust You, Lord, and believe that You are able! Thank You for making me fearless as I rise up with You!

In Jesus' name,
Amen

July 19

*"If anyone would come after me, let him deny himself
and take up his cross and follow me."*
Matthew 16:24

My Prayer

Dear Heavenly Father,

I will follow You, Lord, as You have asked. As I
follow You, I will let go and surrender all to You. All
that I have needed, You have provided. I take up my
cross and follow You to freedom. Thank You for
showing me the way as I obey Your voice. As I listen
to You, the Holy Spirit guides me to all truth. In Your
presence I find fullness of joy! In the stillness of my
soul, I find peace. As I follow You, I find hope! I will
follow You, my Lord!

In Jesus' name,
Amen

July 20

His Promise

*"You hem me in, behind and before, and lay your
hand upon me.'
Psalm 139:5*

My Prayer

Dear Heavenly Father,

Thank You for Your protection over me! You hem
me in behind and before me. I am safe in Your arms
and healed in Your presence. You have rescued me
and given me peace just when I needed help. As I put
my trust in You, I receive Your promised security.
You will never leave or forsake me, this I know! I am
sure of Your love for me and know I am forgiven and
free as one of Your children who has been saved by
grace. I will keep my eyes fixed upon You, my Lord!

In Jesus' name,
Amen

July 21

His Promise

"Speak, Lord, for your servant hears."
1 Samuel 3:9

My Prayer

Dear Heavenly Father,

Thank You for speaking truth to me. I am opening my heart to You. In the stillness of my soul, I hear You. I know You are calling me to come closer and be still. As I do, You will speak to me and fill me with Your purpose. I am listening intently, with faith, to what You need me to do. I cannot wait to see how You will move these mountains! I am ready, my Lord. Speak, for Your servant hears!

In Jesus' name,
Amen

July 22

*"He is not here, for he has risen, as he said.
Come, see the place where he lay."*
Matthew 28:6

My Prayer

Dear Heavenly Father,

You have risen indeed and have given me new life in Christ! I am living in Your promises, and I believe. You live within my heart, and I make my home in You. I am made new with a resurrected heart. Thank You for putting Your Spirit inside me just as You promised. I am free and alive with new life and renewed hope. You have risen, indeed! Praise be to God! Hallelujah!

In Jesus' name,
Amen

July 23

His Promise

"How precious is your steadfast love, O God! The children of mankind take refuge in the shadow of your wings."
Psalm 36:7

My Prayer

Dear Heavenly Father,

Thank You for showing up everywhere I look. I see You in my life and know that You are protecting me in the shadow of Your wings. I am safe in Your presence, Lord! I am showered with hope as I live closer to You. As I believe in Your promises and see them come to life, I am full of joy. I am praying for extra strength and courage that will come from You as I stay connected and committed. My protection comes from You, my Lord, my Defender!

In Jesus' name,
Amen

July 24

"It is more blessed to give than to receive."
Acts 20:35

My Prayer

Dear Heavenly Father,

Thank You for prompting all Your children to give to others. It is truly more blessed to give than to receive! You show up as we obey Your command to love and give from the heart. Your glory is seen in the simple acts of kindness when we let You lead us to share Your love. Your light shines brightly in us as we choose to love others. Your joy grows in us as we think of other people before ourselves. Your blessings abound as we live with giving hearts!

In Jesus' name,
Amen

July 25

"Therefore as the Holy Spirit says, 'Today if you hear his voice, do not harden your hearts as in the day of rebellion, on the day of testing in the wilderness.'"
Hebrews 3:7-8

My Prayer

Dear Heavenly Father,

You have promised to draw near to me. I am clinging to Your promises as I draw near to You. I have hope as I breathe with Your Spirit inside of me. I have faith as I cling to Your love that awakens my soul. I have peace as I am refreshed in Your presence. I have life as I walk with You in the Spirit and listen to Your voice. I have joy as I sing Your praises! Thank You for the renewed hope, faith, peace, and joy that comes only from You, Lord. I am enriched in every way as I come closer to Your love with a softened heart of praise!

In Jesus' name,
Amen

July 26

"Shine as lights in the world, holding fast to the word of life, so that in the day of Christ I may be proud that I did not run in vain or labor in vain."
Philippians 2:15-16

My Prayer

Dear Heavenly Father,

I will shine Your light as I hold on to You and Your Word. You light up my life in a most brilliant way each and every day. Thank You for giving me new life as I open my heart and soul to more of You. There is new hope as I trust You. There is new joy as I keep You close. There is new peace as I rest in Your presence. There is new life as I make my home with You. The darkness has disappeared in the light of Your love. I am shining brightly with new life in You as I hold fast to Your promises, my Lord!

In Jesus' name,
Amen

July 27

"Follow me, I will make you fishers of men."
Matthew 4:19

My Prayer

Dear Heavenly Father,

I will follow You. I am committed to You. Help me, Lord Jesus, to keep going in the direction You show me so that I may be a witness of Your love and grace. I will not be afraid. I will keep the faith as Your child. There is always hope for me when I trust You. Even in the struggles, I will not give up but will press forward with You. I am strong and full of hope as I rely on Your promises. Thank You for letting me see with new eyes as I follow You to freedom and renewed hope!

In Jesus' name,
Amen

July 28

*"The heart of man plans his way, but the Lord
establishes his steps."*
Proverbs 16:9

My Prayer

Dear Heavenly Father,

Thank You for directing my life. I am so confident of
the hope I have in You. I will have security as I spend
more time in Your presence. You want me to draw
near to You so that You can draw near to me. With a
dedicated heart, I will come closer to You. Thank
You for all Your spiritual blessings upon my life. I
am so close to You as I let go and let You lead me to
all truth! I am hopeful for what is to come as I let You
direct my steps!

In Jesus' name,
Amen

July 29

"May he grant you your heart's desire and fulfill all your plans."
Psalm 20:4

My Prayer

Dear Heavenly Father,

Thank You for making all things new! As I pray, I am confident You will watch over me and direct all my plans. I am sure that I will see what You have planned for me. I will open my heart to You and believe. I will praise You with all my being as I see with new eyes of faith. I will wait patiently for You as You work all things out. Thank You for giving me the desires of my heart as I trust You with a grateful heart!

In Jesus' name,
Amen

July 30

His Promise

"And let the peace of Christ rule in your hearts, to which indeed you were called in one body. And be thankful."
Colossians 3:15

My Prayer

Dear Heavenly Father,

You are my peace, Lord. I feel Your peace as I trust You more. Help me to be still so that Your peace will wash over me. It is in Your arms that I will be able to rest. I am praying for peace to invade the hearts of Your people. We all need You, Lord! We can only be at peace in Your presence. Come, Lord Jesus, fill our hearts and souls! We are so thankful for You! Our cups are full with Your perfect peace when You rule in our hearts!

In Jesus' name,
Amen

July 31

"Now to him who is able to do far more abundantly than all that we ask or think, according to the power at work within us."
Ephesians 3:20

My Prayer

Dear Heavenly Father,

I know You will do more in me as I let go and let Your power work in me. Thank You for setting me free so I can let go and fly. I will not be held down any longer by the burdens that have caused me anxiety. I will be free in Your presence as I walk hand in hand with You! My upward faith in You has rescued me and brought me renewed strength and hope. You will do more in me than I could ever imagine if I trust You, first and foremost. Thank You for rescuing me, my Lord, my Redeemer!

In Jesus' name,
Amen

You are my hiding place
and my shield; I hope in
your word.

PSALM 119:114

August 1

"I can do all things through Him who strengthens me."
Philippians 4:13

My Prayer

Dear Heavenly Father,

I am blessed to have You in my life. I will trust You for what You are doing in and through me. Your presence brings me renewed hope and courage. As I keep the faith, You will be my strength. I will not falter but will stay focused on what You are calling me to do. Each step with You brings joy and peace as I step up to each challenge and hold Your promises close to heart. I will not let go of You! I can do all things with You, Lord, as You keep strengthening me day by day!

In Jesus' name,
Amen

August 2

*"And we know that for those who love God all things
work together for good, for those who are called
according to his purpose."*
Romans 8:28

My Prayer

Dear Heavenly Father,

I praise You for working everything out for good even when I do not understand. You have made a way when their seemed to be no way. You have opened doors that I never thought possible. You have given me hope even when things seemed hopeless. You have warmed my heart with Your steadfast love. You have touched my soul with a fresh filling of the Holy Spirit. I am made brand new in You! I will walk with renewed hope, believing You will work all things out for my good and Your glory! Hallelujah!

In Jesus' name,
Amen

August 3

*"Trust in the Lord with all your heart, and do not
lean on your own understanding."*
Proverbs 3:5

My Prayer

Dear Heavenly Father,

You are always patient towards me. Help me to be
patient with Your timing as You are always right on
time to fulfill Your promises to me. I am eagerly
waiting upon You as I trust You with all my heart and
lean not on my own understanding. I know all things
will work out for good as I cling to You and Your
love. Thank You for loving me and giving me the
courage I need as I wait. My strength grows as I cling
tighter to You and not my circumstances. I will
believe even when I cannot yet see what You have
promised me! My faith is alive!

In Jesus' name,
Amen

August 4

"As I live, says the Lord, every knee shall bow to me,
and every tongue shall confess to God."
Romans 14:11

My Prayer

Dear Heavenly Father,

I bow my knees humbly before
You, Lord, confessing my sins
and asking for mercy. You are
the one who can, and will,
forgive me. Thank You for
reaching me with Your love and
saving me by grace. I am whole in
Your presence, and I am forgiven and
free to love as You love. Let my love be
genuine and my actions be pleasing to You, my Lord.
I am letting go and trusting You more and more each
day as I faithfully pray. I praise You for who You are
with all my being!

In Jesus' name,
Amen

August 5

"For he will command his angels concerning you to guard you in all your ways."
Psalm 91:11

My Prayer

Dear Heavenly Father,

You guard me in all Your ways as a child of God. I am so thankful that I know You and have Your protection over me. I am secure and confident in You. Give me peace, my Lord, as I pray. Help me because I need You as the source of strength in my life. I long to be with You. I have Your power when I come closer to Your love. You are my refuge and strength, a very present help in trouble, today and always! I love You, my Lord, my Protector!

In Jesus' name,
Amen

August 6

"For anything that becomes visible is light. Therefore it says, 'Awake, O sleeper, and arise from the dead, and Christ will shine on you.'"
Ephesians 5:14

My Prayer

Dear Heavenly Father,

You want me to arise to new life when I wake up spiritually with Your light shining on me. I have had times of restlessness lately and that is because You want me to be still and listen to You. I do hear Your voice as I pray, encouraging and comforting me. How wonderful it is to have Your Spirit strengthening my soul! I am awake and strong. There is nothing or no one that can take me away from the bright light of Your love and peace!

In Jesus' name,
Amen

August 7

His Promise

"Be kind to one another, tenderhearted, forgiving one another, as God in Christ forgave you."
Ephesians 4:32

My Prayer

Dear Heavenly Father,

I know You have forgiven me and I thank You for this gift of grace. You are so faithful to me, my Lord. I am hearing You speak truth to me about forgiving others. You want me to forgive as You have forgiven me. I will let go of the hurt or offense I am holding in my heart and act with loving kindness. As I do, my burdens will fall away, and my hope will rise. Grace opens the door to the freedom You want to give me. I am free in Christ as I step into grace and let Your love in me flow out to others!

In Jesus' name,
Amen

August 8

*"He heals the brokenhearted
and binds up their wounds."
Psalm 147:3*

My Prayer

Dear Heavenly Father,

I am praying for Your continued healing in my life,
Lord. I know You will bind up my wounds inside and
out. My broken heart will be healed as I come closer
to You. I will reach out to You with my constant and
faithful prayers. Every day with You
in my life is a blessing, indeed! I
will keep praying, believing
Your healing is coming because
You are faithful all the time!

In Jesus' name,
Amen

August 9

"For my yoke is easy, and my burden is light."
Matthew 11:30

My Prayer

Dear Heavenly Father,

Thank You for giving me rest. I am leaning on You to take my burdens and carry them for me. Only You can give me the rest I need as I let go. You have calmed my heart as I rest in Your arms. I am holding You closer on the days that I am restless because I know Your yoke is easy. I will keep trusting You to help me. It is in Your presence where my restlessness turns to peace and my hopelessness turns into joy. I am yoked to You!

In Jesus' name,
Amen

August 10

"Peace be still!"
Mark 4:39

My Prayer

Dear Heavenly Father,

I know You want me to be still. I am praying for peace as I hear You telling me, "Peace be still!' You are a very present help for me. I just need to let go and let You give me peace. I have been fighting this battle all alone and it is time to surrender and let You fight for me. You are ready to take all my burdens to give me peace. I will let go and rest in Your loving arms of peace so that You can settle my soul!

In Jesus' name,
Amen

August 11

His Promise

"Because he holds fast to me in love, I will deliver him; I will protect him, because he knows my name."
Psalm 91:14

My Prayer

Dear Heavenly Father,

I will hold fast to You, my Lord. Your love has given me such hope even in distress. I am calling Your name and asking for help. I know You hear and will deliver me. Thank You for Your promises to protect me. I am standing on Your promises and holding on to hope. I will keep my faith, one day at a time, as I cling tighter to You, my Lord, even in this storm. It is in Your arms that I will find comfort and rest!

In Jesus' name,
Amen

August 12

His Promise

"May the Lord answer you in the day of trouble!'
Psalm 20:1

My Prayer

Dear Heavenly Father,

Answer my cries for help, my Lord! I am lost and weary in this time of trouble. I know You will be there for me whenever I call upon you. Your Word promises me this, and I know Your Word is true. I trust You even when I cannot see. Thank You for reaching me with mercy and gentleness. I need Your touch, Lord. even more right now. I yearn to hear Your soothing voice reminding me that peace is just a prayer away. I will keep waiting patiently as I pray, knowing You will answer me and give me peace. I am still and I hear You!

In Jesus' name,
Amen

August 13

His Promise

"Behold, I am doing a new thing; now it springs forth, do you not perceive it? I will make a way in the wilderness and rivers in the desert."
Isaiah 43:19

My Prayer

Dear Heavenly Father,

I will keep waiting on You, Lord, as I continue trusting and praying patiently. I know You have me waiting to strengthen my faith and make me stronger. I can feel Your peace even in this storm. I will not give up hope but will stand with Your strength supporting me. You have given me fresh hope as I read Your Word and pray. I will keep looking up to see You and thank you for doing something new deep down in my soul. I am made new in Christ with a fresh wind of the Holy Spirit empowering me to endure it all!

In Jesus' name,
Amen

August 14

"Sin will have no dominion over you, since you are not under law but under grace."
Romans 6:14

My Prayer

Dear Heavenly Father,

It is by Your grace that I have been saved. It is a gift from You given freely to me when I believed. I am no longer a slave to sin and bondage, but free to live in peace in Your arms of grace. Thank You for rescuing me all those years ago. Just when I needed You to be my vision in the midst of my blindness and my strength in the midst of my weakness, You picked me up, forgave me, and put new life in me! And still today, You are all these things and so much more to me! I am *all in* for You!

In Jesus' name,
Amen

August 15

"The Lord stood by me and strengthened me, so that through me the message might be fully proclaimed and all the Gentiles might hear it."
2 Timothy 4:17

My Prayer

Dear Heavenly Father,

I will stand because You are standing beside me to strengthen me. I am putting faith over fear as I walk with new power and purpose. Fear has no place in my life as I stand. In times of trouble, You are there. You are my refuge and strength. I feel your presence in the valleys and on the mountaintops. I know You are there in my every moment. I will trust You, my Lord. Greater trust and faith come as I lean on You. Nothing can separate me from Your love!

In Jesus' name,
Amen

August 16

"And it shall come to pass afterward, that I will pour out my Spirit on all flesh; your sons and daughters shall prophesy, your old men shall dream dreams, and your young men shall see visions."
Joel 2:28

My Prayer

Dear Heavenly Father,

Thank You for continuing to pour more of Your Spirit upon all of us. Yet we know there is an outpouring still to come because Your Word gives us this promise. You are so faithful and have shown us Your glory as You renew us spiritually and revive our hearts. We are more than conquerors when You give us new hope. I am standing on Your promises, and I am hopeful for what is to come as I trust You more each day. I will keep believing to receive more of Your Spirit within me! I am alive with the power and strength of the Holy Spirit and awakened to a new, rejuvenated life of joy with You!

In Jesus' name,
Amen

August 17

*"When you pass through the waters,
I will be with you; and through the rivers, they shall
not overwhelm you; when you walk through the fire
you shall not be burned, and the flame shall not
consume you."*
Isaiah 43:2

My Prayer

Dear Heavenly Father,

I will not be afraid because You are always with me. You have been with me from the beginning and will always stay close to me. As I face challenges, You will help me conquer my fears. I will walk hand in hand with You until I see You face to face. And I will not be afraid because I am not alone! I have Your living Spirit flowing through me to guide me. Your Word of life comforts me and gives me new courage. I am not afraid, but am strengthened by You, my Lord! I am strong and courageous!

In Jesus' name,
Amen

August 18

"And hope does not put us to shame, because God's love has been poured into our hearts through the Holy Spirit who has been given to us."
Romans 5:5

My Prayer

Dear Heavenly Father,

Thank You for Your love that has been poured in my heart through the Holy Spirit who you have given me. This gift has touched my soul with utmost joy. I am excited to know Your amazing love as I live connected to You. It is wonderful being close to You, my Lord, and knowing your blessings. As I rest in Your love, I am encouraged and comforted in a special way. It is wonderful to have this hope and experience Your love for me each and every day!

In Jesus' name,
Amen

August 19

"Be steadfast, immovable, always abounding in the work of the Lord."
1 Corinthians 15:58

My Prayer

Dear Heavenly Father,

I will stand firm with You. I will not shrink back but will rise in my faith. I am stronger with You by my side empowering and strengthening me. It is in Your presence where I feel fullness of joy! I am letting go of my burdens and pressing into new opportunities to work for You. Thank You for Your goodness and mercy that are new each and every day. I am grace-filled and full of renewed hope. My future is bright because You light up my life!

In Jesus' name,
Amen

August 20

"Cast your burden on the LORD and he will sustain you."
Psalm 55:22

My Prayer

Dear Heavenly Father,

I will cast my burdens onto You so that You can sustain me. I have been carrying these burdens too long and it is time to surrender all to You. All I need to do is to let go, and You will take them from me. Why do I keep holding on? What am I afraid of? I lift my prayers for bolder faith to You, my Lord. Help me to be strong and courageous with You. It is time to make a difference for You and let my faith rise above my fretting. You will elevate me with hope as I put my trust in You and surrender all!

In Jesus' name,
Amen

August 21

"At the name of Jesus, every knee should bow, in heaven and on earth and under the earth, and every tongue confess that Jesus Christ is Lord, to the glory of God the Father."
Philippians 2:10-11

My Prayer

Dear Heavenly Father,

Oh, Lord, how I love to tell of how great You are as I proclaim You as my Lord and Savior! I trust You wholeheartedly and will listen and obey You. I have heard Your call to love, and I am ready to encourage others as You desire. Even when I cannot understand all of the plan, I can trace Your hand. I know Your power reigns in me as I say "yes" and stay faithful and devoted. I humbly bow my knees to pray and thank You for the gift of Jesus Christ! He is my all in all!

In Jesus' name,
Amen

August 22

"I lift my eyes to the hills. From where does my help come? My help comes from the Lord who made heaven and earth."
Psalm 121:1-2

My Prayer

Dear Heavenly Father,

Help us, Lord! We need You to come touch us with Your healing. We are struggling and need a fresh wave of hope from Your healing hands. We are prayerfully asking for You to touch us with Your love. We need You to reach us and restore us to health physically, mentally, and spiritually like only You can do. We are waiting for You and are praying that You will work in and through us. Give us courage and strength to endure. Help us, O Lord! We know You will rescue us!

In Jesus' name,
Amen

August 23

His Promise

"Each one must give as he has decided in his heart, not reluctantly or under compulsion, for God loves a cheerful giver."
2 Corinthians 9:7

My Prayer

Dear Heavenly Father,

I am so grateful for You in my life! You have reached my heart and touched my soul with Your blessings of great joy. Each day is a gift from You in heaven above. I give You all the glory and praise for Your countless blessings! I will openly show my gratitude by giving back to others with a cheerful heart full of praise. Every day is made for worship of You, my Lord. I will start this day in prayer and praise for Your wonderful promises. I will faithfully follow You. There is new life as a follower of the Way, Jesus Christ! There is new hope as I reach out with Your love and give from a generous heart of praise!

In Jesus' name,
Amen

August 24

"For the LORD is a sun and shield;
the LORD bestows favor and honor. No good thing
does he withhold from those who walk uprightly."
Psalm 84:11

My Prayer

Dear Heavenly Father,

As I pray today, I feel the warmth of Your love covering me. I am praising You for giving me Your grace and protection. Help me to be still and listen as You speak wisdom to me. Your Word gives me peace and hope. Your Spirit of truth has opened the door to greater faith and a closer relationship with You. It is so good to be in Your presence! I feel Your favor over me as I draw to You. I know You are infusing me with strength to rise above any fear as I let go and let You be my shield. Your light shines forever in my heart!

In Jesus' name,
Amen

August 25

"Behold, I am doing a new thing; now it springs
forth, do you not perceive it?"
Isaiah 43:19

My Prayer

Dear Heavenly Father,

I know You are doing something new in me! I do perceive it as I seek more of You. Your presence has encouraged me to press on with hope. I am refreshed by You, my Lord, as I step out in faith. I pray for renewed purpose as I sharpen my spiritual vision to see You. Thank You for the difference You make in my life as I trust You more without even knowing any of the details. I will walk hand in hand with You until I see You face to face!

In Jesus' name,
Amen

244

August 26

His Promise

"Man is like a breath;
his days are like a passing shadow."
Psalm 144:4

My Prayer

Dear Heavenly Father,

I thank You for showing me how I can be closer to You, my Lord. You want me to stay focused on You more as the days pass so I can clearly see You. You call me to be still and know that You are God. I will listen with a grateful heart as You speak. I will make each moment count because the days are passing quickly. Help me to see what You are calling me to do right now. In Your presence, there is fullness of great joy! I am letting go and trusting You more with each passing moment. It is so good to be close to You, my Lord. I am praising You with a joyful heart of hope!

In Jesus' name,
Amen

August 27

"He who is in you is greater than he who is in the world."
1 John 4:4

My Prayer

Dear Heavenly Father,

Oh, how I love You, my Lord! You are the Lord and Savior of my life, and I am so blessed and thankful to know You! You helped me to see when I was blind. You helped me know the way to go when I was confused and needed guidance. You have encouraged me when I needed a friend. I am listening, Lord, speak to me and show me Your glory! You are my all in all who in is all and over all!

In Jesus' name,
Amen

August 28

His Promise

*"Commit your way to the LORD; trust in him,
and he will act."*
Psalm 37:5

My Prayer

Dear Heavenly Father,

I know You will sustain me when I cast my burdens onto You. I am eager to see how You will make a way for me when there seems to be no way. I know You are able! Thank You for showing me how I can be free when I let go and trust You! As I commit my way to You, I know You will act. I have seen You do that for me before, and I am certain You will do it again! What a joy it is to know You love me so much that You will take all my cares and concerns as I release them to You! I am blessed, indeed!

In Jesus' name,
Amen

August 29

*"Let my prayer be counted as incense before you, and
the lifting up of my hands as the evening sacrifice!"*
Psalm 141:2

My Prayer

Dear Heavenly Father,

I lift my heartfelt prayers up to You, my Lord, and
feel connected to You as I pray. You hear my every
word and give close attention to my voice as I lift my
petitions to You. When I pray, I feel Your calming
presence of peace. My problems flee when I find
refuge in Your wings once again. I am resting with
hope as I trust You to answer my prayers in Your
timing and will. You love the sweet aroma of prayer
rising to You. Every prayer is beautiful to You. You
take time to listen to each one. Thank You for giving
me Your perfect peace as I pray in the spirit lifting up
my heart and my hands to You!

In Jesus' name,
Amen

August 30

"So I will bless you as long as I live;
in your name I will lift up my hands."
Psalm 63:4

My Prayer

Dear Heavenly Father,

I will praise You in this storm as I lift my eyes higher to see You. I am looking above my circumstances to You, my Lord. I will bless You no matter what I face because I know You are right beside me helping me each step of the way. I can see clearer as I let go and let You help me. In Your arms I have peace and comfort so I can rest. Your presence gives me protection from whatever comes my way. Thank You for touching me as I reach for You!

In Jesus' name,
Amen

August 31

"But as for me and my house, we will serve the LORD."
Joshua 24:15

My Prayer

Dear Heavenly Father,

You are always there for me, my Lord. I am praying that I will be more devoted to You. As I pray, I hear You asking for more of my heart because You have things to show me. I need to open my ears to hear You and my eyes to see You. As I grow closer to You, I will trust and obey You with a more devoted and faithful heart. I have listened and will return to You, my first love! Today and always, I will serve You, Lord, with gladness and joy!

In Jesus' name,
Amen

I wait for the Lord, my soul waits, and in his word I hope.

PSALM 130:5

September 1

"And a harvest of righteousness is sown in peace by those who make peace."
James 3:18

My Prayer

Dear Heavenly Father,

I know You will bring me peace as I pursue the higher things through You. When I press close to You, my relationship with You gives me a peace that passes all understanding. There are troubles and trials in this life, but I am still called to be a peacemaker. Even when there is no calmness around me, You touch my heart gently and I feel Your reassuring presence. And when Your peace like a river flows through me, it is well with my soul.

In Jesus' name,
Amen

September 2

His Promise

"The LORD is my shepherd; I shall not want."
Psalm 23:1

My Prayer

Dear Heavenly Father,

Thank You for helping me find rest. In You, I have found all that I need. The days ahead of me are complete because I have You close to my heart. I have been restored in Your glorious presence and protection. I will keep being strong with Your guidance and encouragement. I will listen and be obedient to what You are calling me to do, one moment at a time. Speak, Lord, for I am listening. And I am content with You by my side, now and always!

In Jesus' name,
Amen

September 3

"I love you, O LORD, my strength."
Psalm 18:1

My Prayer

Dear Heavenly Father,

Your love has rescued and restored me. I was afraid, but because I trusted You, I am fearless. You are my ever-present help in trouble and my strength to keep persevering. I am grateful for Your love that gives me confidence. I will bless and honor You with all that I do. I will praise You with all that is within me as I become braver and stronger with each passing day in Your presence!

In Jesus' name,
Amen

September 4

"Trust in him at all times, O people; pour out your heart before him; God is a refuge for us."
Psalm 62:8

My Prayer

Dear Heavenly Father,

As I wait in silence, I will trust You. Help me as I keep praying patiently and fervently for Your help and direction. I am truly blessed by Your mighty hand of comfort and peace. Calm my heart once again, Lord, for I am weary. These things that I did not expect have risen up against me. But I will let my faith rise above my fear as I trust you. I am pouring my heart out to You with renewed hope and expectant faith to see You work miracles! I do believe Your promises and I will stay in Your refuge!

In Jesus' name,
Amen

September 5

"Let me dwell in your tent forever! Let me take refuge under the shelter of your wings!"
Psalm 61:4

My Prayer

Dear Heavenly Father,

I am tired and weary from all the worry. As I pray today, I surrender all my fears, worries, and doubts to You, my Lord! In times of uncertainty, I will keep praying and trusting. I can find true rest knowing I have found shelter in Your wings. As I take refuge in You, a perfect peace finds me and touches my soul. A new fire of passion begins to spark in my heart as I let go and listen to Your voice calming me. My mind is at rest in this sweet surrender. I will let You be in control of me as I dwell in Your tent where I will remain with You forever!

In Jesus' name,
Amen

September 6

His Promise

"O my Strength, I will sing praises to you, for you, O God, are my fortress, the God who shows me steadfast love."
Psalm 59:17

My Prayer

Dear Heavenly Father,

You, O God, are my fortress and strength! I am sure of Your love for me— A love that endures for eternity. Nothing can separate me from Your love! I will remain strong in Your refuge as I pray for endurance today. There are many things I do not have control over, but one thing I can do is pray and keep my faith alive. I choose to remain faithful to You and love You with my whole heart. You are my source of strength, power, and love that remains forever!

In Jesus' name,
Amen

September 7

"When I am afraid, I put my trust in you."
Psalm 56:3

My Prayer

Dear Heavenly Father,

There are so many things that have been on my mind. Fear tries to set in when I take my mind off You. I will let go of the negative things and put my firm trust in You, my Lord. I know You will help me when I let go. You are my refuge and strength, a very present help in trouble. Thank You for the faith that swells within me. Help me to seek You with all my heart and not lean on my own understanding. In all my ways, Lord, I will acknowledge You so that You can make me fearless!

In Jesus' name,
Amen

September 8

"I will praise you with an upright heart, when I learn your righteous rules."
Psalm 119:7

My Prayer

Dear Heavenly Father,

I can feel Your Spirit warming my heart as I sit still before You. Your love is so wonderful, and Your grace is so amazing, my Lord! I will praise You every day for Your enduring love that has touched every part of me. Your love enriches and awakens the deep desires of my heart and soul. How precious is Your unconditional love! How wonderful is Your love for me! Your love has awakened and renewed me! I am rejoicing that You are my Lord and Savior because I made the decision to believe!

In Jesus' name,
Amen

September 9

"Rejoice in hope, be patient in tribulation,
be constant in prayer."
Romans 12:12

My Prayer

Dear Heavenly Father,

Thank You for the hope You give me. I rejoice and remain constant in prayer. I know You will always be by my side no matter what I face. Your love conquers all my fears and wipes away my tears. I am grateful for Your love that never ends! I am praising You for this love and I will maintain the hope that You bring to me today and always!

In Jesus' name,
Amen

September 10

His Promise

*"Bless the LORD O my soul! O LORD my God, you
are very great! You are clothed with splendor and
majesty!"*
Psalm 104:1

My Prayer

Dear Heavenly Father,

You are so wonderful, Lord! Thank You for standing
by me and strengthening me! Whenever I need You,
You are there. I will keep focusing on You and Your
steadfast love for me! Each day I am stronger in Your
presence. I will keep my faith as I lift my spiritual
eyes to see You clearer. I will listen as I pray to hear
Your voice calm my fears and comfort me through it
all. I will stand stronger with You by my side, now
and forever!

In Jesus' name,
Amen

September 11

His Promise

"Whoever has my commandments and keeps them, he it is who loves me. And he who loves me will be loved by my Father, and I will love him and manifest myself to him."
John 14:21

My Prayer

Dear Heavenly Father,

I am praising You for Your love! It is amazing to know You and Your love, Lord! I will obey You as You desire because my desire is to please You. I will show my love for You by walking in obedience and faith. You have shown Yourself mightily to all who love You and walk in obedience following Your commandments. I will listen, trust, and obey You. I am excited for what is to come when I see You working in me. I love You with all that is in me, my Lord!

In Jesus' name,
Amen

September 12

"The righteous shall live by faith."
Romans 1:17

My Prayer

Dear Heavenly Father,

I will live by faith. My whole life is in Your hands. The faith I acquired in the beginning when I first found You and believed, to the faith I have now that is strong and continuing to grow is an enduring, one-step-at-a-time faith that helps me rise above challenges in my life, O Lord. I desire You in all areas of my life. I desire a sincere and steady faith as You mold me into who You need and want me to be. And because I have been promised eternal life as Your faith-filled child, Lord, I desire an everlasting faith. From faith to faith, right by You, my Lord and Savior!

In Jesus' name,
Amen

September 13

"...prayed for them that they might receive the Holy Spirit."
Acts 8:15

My Prayer

Dear Heavenly Father,

You want us to keep praying for all to receive the Holy Spirit. I will pray and faithfully believe even when I do not yet see how this work will come to fruition. As we each believe in Jesus, surrender our old self, and love You with all our heart, we will receive the promised Holy Spirit who will change us and give us a renewed and transformed life. Yes, You have promised this gift to all who will receive You! It is our choice to believe and surrender our control over to You, Lord and Savior of our souls. We are empowered with the Holy Spirit when we say yes to You! I will say Amen for this glorious truth that I am standing on forevermore!

In Jesus' name,
Amen

September 14

"And let us run with endurance the race that is set before us, looking to Jesus, the founder and perfecter of our faith, who for the joy that was set before him endured the cross, despising the shame, and is seated at the right hand of the throne of God."
Hebrews 12:1-2

My Prayer

Dear Heavenly Father,

I will look to You for endurance as I run my race. As I keep my eyes fixed on You, I will know the steps to take. I will not take my eyes off You but will run with endurance because You are in my sight. I know You have promised me an abundant life of joy when I keep the faith. With You present in me, I will press on with new hope and strength. The road is narrow and long with multiple decisions and challenges to face, but the race is not impossible with You, Jesus, the source and the perfecter of my faith!

In Jesus' name,
Amen

September 15

His Promise

"Blessed are the eyes that see what you see!"
Luke 10:23

My Prayer

Dear Heavenly Father,

I will see clearly when I focus on You, my Lord! I want to see the needs of others with my spiritual eyes. I will take off my blinders and look with eyes of grace. I will put on love and spread it with joy. I am ready to make a difference for You, Lord. And I will see the awe and wonder of what You want to show me when I seek Your will and walk in Your way. I am blessed with eyes to see as I say "yes" and choose to let it be!

In Jesus' name,
Amen

September 16

*"You also must be ready for the Son of Man is
coming at an hour you do not expect."*
Luke 12:40

My Prayer

Dear Heavenly Father,

I know You will come again because You have
promised me this in Your word! I must be ready in
my heart and with my actions. I will live
out my faith so that You will find me to
be faithful when You come. I will keep
obeying Your word so I can stay
focused on You, my Promised
Savior. I will keep working towards
the goal of a closer relationship with
You, my Lord, because You bring
me such joy! Each day is a blessing
for me to be able to share it with
You. Thank You for being faithful
to me all the days of my life!

In Jesus' name,
Amen

September 17

"But who do you say that I am?"
Mark 8:29

My Prayer

Dear Heavenly Father,

You are my Lord and my Savior! I am connected and close to You. As I ponder all You are to me, I am praising You and so thankful for Your Holy Spirit within me. It is in the still moments where I keep my focus on You, that I can hear Your voice speaking truth to me. You are my Wonderful Counselor. When I need direction, You are my Way Maker and Miracle Worker. I have many ways I could go, but only one way that leads to life everlasting! You are my Way! I love You, my Redeemer and my Living Hope!

In Jesus' name,
Amen

September 18

"And walk in love, as Christ loved us and gave himself up for us, a fragrant offering and sacrifice to God."
Ephesians 5:2

My Prayer

Dear Heavenly Father,

I need to stop talking the talk and start walking the walk. Help me to love like You desire. I need direction as I live out what You have spoken to me. I commit to love so my heart can be open to what You are telling me to do. You gave of yourself with sacrifice so that I could be free from sin and live out the gospel message with unconditional love to those around me. Your sweet smell has permeated all the areas of my life now that I am Yours! I am walking in the sweetness of Your love, and it is well with my soul!

In Jesus' name,
Amen

September 19

His Promise

*"Do not be anxious about anything, but in everything
by prayer and supplication with thanksgiving let your
requests be made known to God."*
Philippians 4:6

My Prayer

Dear Heavenly Father,

Thank You for taking care of me as I let go
of my anxiety and burdens. I am giving
them all to You. There is nothing I can do
about these things which I have no
control, so I will let go and let You work
all things out in Your will. I trust You
with all my heart. You have promised to
wipe away all my tears and remove my
fears if I trust You. I will continue praying
and believing You will take all my cares when
I cast them to You. It is good to know Your
enduring love for me. As I wait, I will keep my
head up and my faith strong. I give You all of
me so that You can do Your work in me.

In Jesus' name,
Amen

September 20

"Finally, brothers, whatever is true, whatever is honorable, whatever is just, whatever is pure, whatever is lovely, whatever is commendable, if there is any excellence, if there is anything worthy of praise, think about these things."
Philippians 4:8

My Prayer

Dear Heavenly Father,

Help me to speak truth, hope, and encouragement that comes from You, O Lord. Direct my thoughts and my mind with goodness and love that flows only from You. Guide my steps as I walk in faith and live out what You have put on my heart. I will keep close to You as I think about things that are true, lovely, pure, worthy, and commendable in your sight. I will look to You, the Author of my life and Founder of my faith. You have written the most beautiful words in the scriptures for me to speak to others in love. Guide me, Lord Jesus, my Rock, out of Your perfect love!

In Jesus' name,
Amen

September 21

"He who calls you is faithful; he will surely do it."
1 Thessalonians 5:24

My Prayer

Dear Heavenly Father,

I know You will do what You promise because You are always faithful! Help me to remain faithful to You, and help grow my faith even in times of uncertainty and doubt. You ask that I trust You and walk by faith and not by sight. I will obey without seeing all the details. I hear You calling me. I believe in Your promises to me. I will go as You lead me. All that I need You will provide. I know that You, my Lord, will surely do it! Great is Your faithfulness unto me!

In Jesus' name,
Amen

September 22

*"When the Spirit of truth comes,
he will guide you into all the truth."*
John 16:13

My Prayer

Dear Heavenly Father,

Thank You for the truth! I know You will guide me into all truth when I trust You. I will acknowledge You in all my ways and find comfort knowing You are guiding me. I may not see the details, but I will trust You anyway. You have given me the truth found in Your Word. I will obey, as You instruct me, with the guidance and power of the Holy Spirit inside me. Where Your Spirit is, there is freedom! I am listening to the promptings of the Holy Spirit, Lord! Keep speaking truth to me!

In Jesus' name,
Amen

September 23

*"And above all these, put on love, which binds
everything together in perfect harmony."*
Colossians 3:14

My Prayer

Dear Heavenly Father,

I know You want us to live in unity with Your love
binding us together. In these times in which we live,
there are distractions that try to pull us away from
You. But as we love one another, Your love will hold
everything together in perfect harmony. I will put on
Your love and keep drawing closer to You as I abide
in You more day by day. I will aim to love others
with grace as You have loved me. I am humbled by
how much You love me, Lord! Your love is so patient
and kind and full of grace. I will keep faithfully
loving You as I give my whole heart to You, and I
will continue to steadfastly pray for harmony for all
Your people. More of Your love is the key to
harmony!

In Jesus' name,
Amen

September 24

*"Continue steadfastly in prayer,
being watchful in it with thanksgiving."*
Colossians 4:2

My Prayer

Dear Heavenly Father,

Oh, Lord, how I love knowing You hear all my prayers, every single one of them! I am so thankful for Your faithfulness to me even as I wait for answers. I will be patient and stay encouraged as I know You want the best for me and those on my heart. You are listening and will answer. I will not give up and will continue steadfastly praying with a grateful heart. Lord, thank You for lighting up my life with new hope and joy and an expectation of what is to come. I believe the best is yet to come as I stay close to You!

In Jesus' name,
Amen

September 25

His Promise

*"The LORD is near to the brokenhearted and saves
the crushed in spirit."*
Psalm 34:18

My Prayer

Dear Heavenly Father,

I know You are near to me, my Lord, because I feel Your presence. Thank You for hearing my prayers and healing me. You have healed me inside and out. I am made whole by You, my Lord. What was broken, You have healed. What was lost, has been found in You. What was weakened, You have restored. All that I need, You have provided. Great is Your faithfulness to me! I will be faithful to You with a new song in my heart and soul!

In Jesus' name,

Amen

September 26

"Abide in me, and I in you. As the branch cannot bear fruit by itself, unless it abides in the vine, neither can you, unless you abide in me."
John 15:4

My Prayer

Dear Heavenly Father,

I know You want me to abide in You, my Lord! I have seen wonderful evidence of You all over my life. I will abide with You, Lord, and keep moving forward as You continue to enrich me. I will stay strong as I stay connected. You give me incredible power and peace when I trust You even more each day. You give me fresh faith as I make You a priority. The eyes of my heart are full of wonder and awe as I abide more in Your presence. With each new morning, I am washed in mercy from You. I am alive and filled with greater hope!

In Jesus' name,
Amen

September 27

His Promise

"For it is God who works in you, both to will and to work for his good pleasure."
Philippians 2:13

My Prayer

Dear Heavenly Father,

Thank You for working in me, Lord, to do Your will for Your good pleasure. I am humbled and graced to do Your will. I am stronger and wiser when You are alive within me. I will not be defeated because I know You are helping me. I am listening to You and will follow You as You call me. I will go because You lead me. Thank You for picking me up when I am weak and infusing me with Your power. Your glory shines brightly within me as I trust and obey You more and more. My whole heart is Yours, my Lord and my Redeemer!

In Jesus' name,
Amen

September 28

His Promise

*"And I will give you a new heart, and a new spirit I
will put within you. And I will remove the heart of
stone from your flesh and give you a heart of flesh."*
Ezekiel 36:26

My Prayer

Dear Heavenly Father,

I am praying for restoration for all who are seeking
more of You. Put a new heart within us and give us
more of Your Spirit to come alive inside us. We are a
people who have been spiritually sleepwalking and
have hardened our hearts at times. We need to return
to You with our whole hearts and souls. Help us to
come closer to Your love and grace. Soften our hearts
and revive our souls. This world has tried to
overcome us, but we know that You came to conquer
our fears and overcome this world. He who is in us is
greater than he who is in the world! Let us cling
tighter to You to shine brighter! Revive and restore us
again to Yourself!

In Jesus' name,
Amen

September 29

His Promise

"By grace you have been saved."
Ephesians 2:5

My Prayer

Dear Heavenly Father,

Thank You for saving me! By Your grace, I have been saved. I know this grace is a gift from You and I am humbled to receive it. My joy spills over as I walk in freedom with You. I am basking in the everlasting joy that comes from You. Thank You for forgiving me so that I may have hope once again. My salvation has set me free, and Your grace is sufficient for me!

In Jesus' name,
Amen

September 30

"Because he holds fast to me in love, I will deliver him; I will protect him, because he knows my name."
Psalm 91:14

My Prayer

Dear Heavenly Father,

I know you are calling my name and waiting patiently on me to listen. I hear You, Lord! I will respond to You when You call. Hear my prayers, Lord. I need You to help me and guide me! I am trying to battle things on my own, but You want me to let You fight my battles. You will protect and defend me as I let go and let You. Thank You, Lord, for being my present help in trouble and my refuge and strength always!

In Jesus' name,
Amen

...but the Lord takes
pleasure in those who fear
him, in those who hope in
his steadfast love.

PSALM 147:11

October 1

"And he said to him, 'Well done, good servant!'"
Luke 19:17

My Prayer

Dear Heavenly Father,

You have given me opportunities to shine Your light. I am pressing into You with my full trust so that You can show me the way. I will commit my way to You, by faith, one step at a time. It is so good to know You will help me every step of the way. I want to be Your faithful servant, my Lord. I want to please you more and more. I am growing in grace as I live out my faith for Your glory!

In Jesus' name,
Amen

October 2

"The apostles said to the Lord, 'Increase our faith!'"
Luke 17:5

My Prayer

Dear Heavenly Father,

I need You, Lord! Help my unbelief and increase my faith! My joy comes from the choice of letting You live in me. I will walk closely with You and with joy inside me. These days are full of burdens and challenges, but with You, I can overcome them all! I know that You will fight my battles. I just need to let go and let You do it! Thank You for giving me hope as my faith increases. I do believe!

In Jesus' name,
Amen

October 3

"And let us consider how to stir up one another to love and good works."
Hebrews 10:24

My Prayer

Dear Heavenly Father,

I want to be a good example to point people to You. I pray that I can love others like You do. With Your love, I can be all that You want me to be. I will encourage others. Your love gives me hope that I can spread to those around me, and my faith will grow stronger as I grow closer to You. I will continue stirring others up to love and good works. I am content with You in me. There is always a light of hope when I cling to You!

In Jesus' name,
Amen

October 4

His Promise

*"Blessed rather are those who hear the word of God
and keep it!"*
Luke 11:28

My Prayer

Dear Heavenly Father,

I know You want me to obey Your Word and believe
Your wonderful promises. You have blessed me, and
I keep Your Word close to my heart. As I pray today,
I know You are listening and will answer my
petitions I present to You. Before I ask, You know
what I need. I hear Your commands and I will obey.
Thank You for blessing me. I am humbled and graced
to have a relationship with You. I am blessed, indeed!

In Jesus' name,
Amen

October 5

"I the LORD do not change."
Malachi 3:6

My Prayer

Dear Heavenly Father,

Thank You for never changing. You are the same yesterday, today, and always. I know that Your love is constant and endless. I am encouraged and believe all Your promises to me. Changes surround me, but You, O Lord, never change! I am grateful for Your love, and I have faith in You and all Your promises!

In Jesus' name,
Amen

October 6

"And as you wish that others would do to you,
do so to them."
Luke 6:31

My Prayer

Dear Heavenly Father,

Help me to be patient with others. I know You want me to treat others with love and respect. You want me to give grace as You have given me. You ask that I strive to live peacefully with all. Even though it can be hard at times to be patient, with Your help, I will aim to love with a pure heart, a good conscience, and a sincere faith. I will patiently show love and kindness to others because Your presence is alive and active in me!

In Jesus' name,
Amen

October 7

*"Why are you cast down, O my soul, and why are you
in turmoil within me? Hope in God; for I shall again
praise him, my salvation and my God."*
Psalm 42:5

My Prayer

Dear Heavenly Father,

I will find my hope in You, my Lord, my hope of
glory! I will have faith in You even when I cannot
see. I will be strong in You so that You can show me
Your glory. The problems I face will help me grow in
my faith. With You present in me, I can overcome
anything. Fear and worry disappear when I cling to
You and not the world. You are my freedom and my
salvation from sin. Nothing or no one can separate me
from Your everlasting love and peace! I am alive in
Christ!

In Jesus' name,
Amen

October 8

"The promises of God find their Yes in him. That is why it is through him that we utter Amen to God for his glory."
2 Corinthians 1:20

My Prayer

Dear Heavenly Father,

I believe in Your promises! I will say Amen time and time again to Your amazing promises. You are to be praised for the wonderful ways You speak truth and life into me. I am marveling at all the ways You love me! It is wonderful to know Your love and I praise You for Your numerous promises! Thank You for loving me like You do! I love You!

In Jesus' name,
Amen

October 9

His Promise

"But the fruit of the Spirit is love, joy, peace, patience, kindness, goodness, faithfulness, gentleness, self-control; against such things there is no law."
Galatians 5:22-23

My Prayer

Dear Heavenly Father,

I pray for more of Your Spirit in me. Thank You for giving me the fruit of the Spirit as I seek more of Your presence in my life. And I know You bring me gifts and talents so I can bear more fruit for You. I am so thankful I have Your Spirit active and alive in me! Every day You bless my life with these gifts of the Spirit. There is no law against these spiritual fruits. As I bear much fruit, You bring me so much joy! I am so thankful and so abundantly blessed by You!

In Jesus' name,
Amen

October 10

His Promise

"For the sake of Christ, then, I am content with weaknesses, insults, hardships, persecutions, and calamities. For when I am weak, then I am strong."
2 Corinthians 12:10

My Prayer

Dear Heavenly Father,

In my weakness, You will be my strength! Help me to draw closer to You in the challenges that I face. I know when I am weak, you are strong. I know what it means to have hardships and feel weak. I have experienced Your grace time and time again and I am encouraged each time. I will let Your power become active in me as I am empowered with new life from You. My life is enriched with Your powerful Spirit. Thank You for the strength You give me! I am strong in You!

In Jesus' name,
Amen

October 11

"God is faithful, by whom you were called into the fellowship of his Son, Jesus Christ our Lord."
Corinthians 1:9

My Prayer

Dear Heavenly Father,

I know You are always faithful! Thank You for keeping me safe even in the storms. You are so wonderful, Lord! You have promised to be faithful to me. I will remain faithful to You in all circumstances even when I cannot see all the details. You know how it will all work out and that is so comforting to me. All I need to do is trust You in all my ways and not lean on my own understanding. You will direct my path as I walk by faith! Not all have faith, but You, O Lord, are faithful!

In Jesus' name,
Amen

October 12

*"For as the heavens are higher than the earth, so are
my ways higher than your ways and my thoughts than
your thoughts."*
Isaiah 55:9

My Prayer

Dear Heavenly Father,

I believe You want me to keep trusting You
no matter what I see. You always know the
best plan for me. I hear You telling me,
"Keep Your faith, do not let go of me. For I
know the perfect plans I have for you that
will be fulfilled when You keep trusting
and obeying me." I will continue on this
path of faith with Your mighty power
guiding me. I hear Your gentle whisper of
love guiding me into all truth and wisdom. I
will not let go of You. I have peace in Your
presence!

In Jesus' name,
Amen

October 13

"For I, the LORD your God, hold your right hand; it is I who say to you, 'Fear not, I am the one who helps you.'"
Isaiah 41:13

My Prayer

Dear Heavenly Father,

You are God almighty! I love You so much! I am not afraid as I hold Your hand. You will help me with what I need if I trust You through it all. With this trust, I have extra strength and power to get through anything that comes my way. Thank You for showing me Your goodness and mercy all the days of my life! I am holding You close to my heart today and forevermore! There is no fear when You are near, Lord!

In Jesus' name,
Amen

October 14

His Promise

"Who shall separate us from the love of Christ? Shall tribulation, or distress, or persecution, or famine, or nakedness, or danger or sword?"
Romans 8:35

My Prayer

Dear Heavenly Father,

Your love is so wonderful! I am so full of life because I have You on my mind and in my heart. Thank You for loving me so much! You have brought so much joy to my life even in the challenges. You have renewed my hope and restored my soul. I am basking in Your everlasting love. Thank You for reaching me with Your unending love, time and time again. I am free in You, my Lord! I am loved by You, my Prince of Peace! Nothing can separate me from You!

In Jesus' name,
Amen

October 15

"Therefore, as you have received Christ Jesus the Lord, so walk in him, rooted and built up in him and established in the faith, just as you were taught, abounding in thanksgiving."
Colossians 2:6-7

My Prayer

Dear Heavenly Father,

I will keep close to You, my Lord. I am walking with You so You can lead me where You want me to go. As I stay close, I am rooted and grounded in Your love. All my fears vanish when You are near. I see Your light when I walk with You and let the Spirit lead me. Thank You for showing me the way. I pray for all of us to grow our faith even more, Lord, as we establish ourselves in You. Our faith will grow deeper when we are rooted in Your good soil of faith. I am so thankful for what You are doing in all who walk in You. Our faith will grow deeper! Hallelujah!

In Jesus' name,
Amen

October 16

"Surely goodness and mercy shall follow me all the days of my life, and I shall dwell in the house of the LORD forever."

My Prayer

Dear Heavenly Father,

You have given me so many wonderful blessings of joy! I am grateful for all of them as I pray today. Thank You for being my shepherd. I will follow You. I will keep trusting and obeying You as I love You with all my heart. You want me to keep You close at heart all the days of my life. I shall not want when I have all I need in You! Thank You for giving me more than I could ever ask for! I am grateful and humbled by Your love and grace over me!

In Jesus' name,
Amen

October 17

"If we live by the Spirit, let us also keep in step with the Spirit."
Galatians 5:25

My Prayer

Dear Heavenly Father,

I am filled with the Spirit. Thank You for leading me. I will listen to You and keep in step with the Spirit as I obey. You have given me wonderful blessings. I have life as I set my mind on the Spirit. I have the fruit of the Spirit of love, joy, peace, patience, kindness, goodness, faithfulness, gentleness, and self-control. All of these gifts flow from a life in the Spirit. I will continue being led by the Spirit so that I can see You alive in me!

In Jesus' name,
Amen

October 18

His Promise

"For freedom Christ has set us free; stand firm therefore, and do not submit again to a yoke of slavery."
Galatians 5:1

My Prayer

Dear Heavenly Father,

You are so amazing, Lord! Thank You for the freedom that is found in You! I will stand firm in this freedom that is mine in Christ. You have promised me so much. As I lean on Your promises, I will remember that all Your promises have their *Yes* in You. I will stand firmly on Your promises so I can experience a deeper relationship with greater freedom. My relationship with You grows with every faithful step I take closer to You! I am free!

In Jesus' name,
Amen

October 19

His Promise

*"But Jesus came and touched them, saying,
'Rise, and have no fear.'"*
Matthew 17:7

My Prayer

Dear Heavenly Father,

I need You to help me. I have been
afraid and need You. I know that Your
touch will heal me inside and out.
You tell me to rise and have no fear
because Your touch heals. The fear
around me does not come from You.
It will disappear when I rise and
follow You, my Lord. Thank You
for helping me. All I have to do is ask
and You will be there! I am trusting You
completely!

In Jesus' name,
Amen

October 20

His Promise

"If any of you lacks wisdom, let him ask God, who gives generously without reproach, and it will be given him."
James 1:5

My Prayer

Dear Heavenly Father,

As I pray today, I realize that You have been producing steadfastness in me. I have gone through various trials that have tested me but produced greater faith within me. Even in those times, Your hand was upon me giving me wisdom. Even in the challenges, You were there with open arms. Your love has remained. You never left me. You were just waiting, yes, waiting for me to come to You with my whole heart and believe. I believe to receive all You have for me!

In Jesus' name,
Amen

October 21

*"In the same way, let your light shine before others,
so that they may see your good works and give glory
to your Father who is in heaven."*
Matthew 5:16

My Prayer

Dear Heavenly Father,

I need more of You! The world tries to pull my attention away from You. There are distractions all around me. Help me to be a light and not dwell in the darkness around me. I will draw to Your light so that I can see who needs me. Many people are searching for hope these days. Open my eyes to see beyond my problems so that I can help where You need me. I know I was called to serve You! I will rise and stand firm with You, my Lord, my hope of glory!

In Jesus' name,
Amen

October 22

His Promise

"Hear my prayer, O Lord;
give ear to my pleas for mercy!"
Psalm 143:1

My Prayer

Dear Heavenly Father,

I know that You are close to me. As I pray today, I want to ask for more mercy. Hear my pleas for mercy, Lord! You know how much I need You in my life. I thank You for loving and forgiving me. My soul is at peace knowing Your grace is enough. You bring abundant joy to my life! I do not need to worry or fear because You are near!

In Jesus' name ,
Amen

October 23

His Promise

"When I am afraid, I put my trust in you. In God, whose word I praise, in God I trust; I shall not be afraid. What can flesh do to me?"
Psalm 56:3-4

My Prayer

Dear Heavenly Father,

I will not let fear control me. I am not afraid when I put my trust in You alone. You give me courage and help in all circumstances. In You, I place my trust. Fear has no place in my heart. I am strong and courageous with You by my side. Thank You for giving me renewed strength for the journey. There is joy in my life as I walk with You, Lord, now and forevermore! I am courageous and fearless, and You enrich my soul!

In Jesus' name,
Amen

October 24

His Promise

"O LORD, I call upon you; hasten to me!
Give ear to my voice when I call to you!"
Psalm 141:1

My Prayer

Dear Heavenly Father,

I know You hear me as I call to You. My prayer,
Lord, is for guidance and direction. I give You my
utmost attention so I can hear You. I know You will
speak truth to me. Thank You for
being my compass so that I can
know which way to go. You are
truly leading me to the best way
to go; this I know! Speak, Lord,
for Your servant is listening!

In Jesus' name,
Amen

October 25

"And whatever you ask in prayer,
you will receive if you have faith."
Matthew 21:22

My Prayer

Dear Heavenly Father,

I am before You asking that You help me. I lift my prayers faithfully to You, believing You will answer. I know You always hear me when I pray. My heart is heavy as I come before You. Forgive me for the ways I have disappointed You. I am ready to follow You to hope and freedom and surrender what has been holding me back from a closer relationship with You, my Lord. I hear Your voice calling me to lay aside all the weight of sin and walk by the Spirit. As I live by faith, I will see more than I could ever dream or imagine just as You have promised me! I am excited for what lies ahead! I believe!

In Jesus' name,
Amen

October 26

"For this reason, make every effort to supplement your faith with virtue, and virtue with knowledge."
2 Peter 1:5

My Prayer

Dear Heavenly Father,

I want to grow more in my faith. Help me to remain faithful by continuing to stay on the path of righteousness with You. I know You will help me increase my faith as I trust You and Your Word. You are doing a new thing in me, and I perceive it! I will walk in the way You direct me, one step at a time, as I commit and supplement my faith with virtue! The best is yet to come!

In Jesus' name,
Amen

October 27

His Promise

"By Your endurance you will gain your lives."
Luke 21:19

My Prayer

Dear Heavenly Father,

You are the one who will give me eternal hope as I press on with you. I will gain life as I stay connected to You, my life source. I am grateful for all that You are doing in me. I am stronger because You live in me. Help me to listen to You and obey what You need me to do. I am stronger when I keep You close at heart. Your love is carrying me and holding me close. I am at peace in Your presence!

In Jesus' name,
Amen

October 28

His Promise

"On the day I called, you answered me;
my strength of soul you increased."
Psalm 138:3

My Prayer

Dear Heavenly Father,

I need strength for life's challenges. There are things weighing heavily on me that only You know. I am surrendering all to You so that You can increase my strength of soul. I am waiting patiently upon You, my Lord. I need You and will keep praying fervently as I draw closer to You in every moment. As I speak to You and hear Your voice, I am content with peace. My soul is free because You live in me!

In Jesus' name,
Amen

October 29

"These things I have spoken to you, that my joy may be in you, and that your joy may be full."
John 15:11

My Prayer

Dear Heavenly Father,

I know Your joy because I know You! Only You can bring the lasting joy that remains in me. Thank You for wrapping me in Your love as I cling closer to You. I am full and alive inside because of Your radiant joy that lives inside me. It is so good to know You, my Lord, as I continue walking in relationship with You. Nothing can steal my joy when I center my life and focus on You!

In Jesus' name,
Amen

October 30

His Promise

"And when they had prayed, the place in which they were gathered together was shaken, and they were all filled with the Holy Spirit and continued to speak the word of God with boldness."
Acts 4:31

My Prayer

Dear Heavenly Father,

I will speak with boldness as I am filled with the Holy Spirit. I will live out my faith and I listen and obey You. I will stand up for what is right and just. Thank You for strengthening me each moment. I have faith and endurance for what You need me to do for You. I have changed because I have Your power actively working in me. I am filled with new hope because I am new in Christ! Hallelujah!

In Jesus' name,
Amen

October 31

"Having purified your souls by your obedience to the truth for a sincere brotherly love, love one another earnestly from a pure heart."
1 Peter 1:22

My Prayer

Dear Heavenly Father,

You have called me to love as You love. You want me to show love that comes from a pure heart. I am most grateful for Your love! I am holding You close at heart so that I can shine Your love on others around me. I know this perfect love that flows from You because I have a close relationship with You. I am free to live in love as I love You!

In Jesus' name,
Amen

May the God of hope fill you with all joy and peace in believing, so that by the power of the Holy Spirit you may abound in hope.

ROMANS 15:13

November 1

"I praise the LORD as long as I live; I will sing praises to my God while I have my being."
Psalm 146:2

My Prayer

Dear Heavenly Father,

I will sing praises to You, my God and Savior! You have given me renewed hope as I cling to You. I will faithfully follow You and trust You wherever You lead me. You have restored and brought me new life. I fruitfully grow in my relationship with You. Thank You, Lord, for the miracles I see as I open my heart to more of the Holy Spirit's power growing beautifully within me!

In Jesus' name,
Amen

November 2

"Peace to you!"
Luke 24:36

My Prayer

Dear Heavenly Father:

Thank You for giving me peace! You are the peace that passes all understanding. I am so thankful for You! I will draw to You more and more so that I can feel Your peace wash over me. Today I am full of hope as I come closer to You! Only You are my peace! I am still in Your presence!

In Jesus' name,
Amen

November 3

"That whoever who believes in Him may have eternal life."
John 3:15

My Prayer

Dear Heavenly Father,

I pray that all would choose to believe! You have given everyone who believes the gift of eternal life. I am so thankful for this gift. I pray for all to receive You and find eternal life. It is so good to know this life that is found in You! I am thankful and blessed to know You as my Lord and Savior! You have changed me! I am clinging to Your promises and pondering Your peace, goodness, and grace You have given me and all who believe!

In Jesus' name,
Amen

November 4

His Promise

"But I have prayed for you that your faith may not fail. And when you have turned again, strengthen your brothers."
Luke 22:32

My Prayer

Dear Heavenly Father,

I am praying for greater faith. As I grow in my faith, I will act in ways that please You. It is so good to see You at work in me. I am growing through my challenges one step of faith at a time. Help me to keep my faith alive as I aim to strengthen those around me as well. I delight in You and live with active faith alive in me!

In Jesus' name,
Amen

November 5

His Promise

"In Him was life, and life was the light of men."
John 1:4

My Prayer

Dear Heavenly Father,

I have life in You. Your light shines in me because I have decided to follow You. There is an inexpressible and glorious joy that awaits me when I trust You with all my heart. I see hope in every step I take with You. You light up my path as I draw closer to You. Thank You for giving me life, my Lord! I am keeping You close at heart all the days of my life! You light up my life!

In Jesus' name,
Amen

November 6

His Promise

"Jesus said to her, 'Everyone who drinks of this water will be thirsty again, but whoever drinks of the water that I will give him will never be thirsty again. The water that I will give him will become in him a spring of water welling up to eternal life.'"
John 4:13

My Prayer

Dear Heavenly Father,

I know You will give me courage and strength to continue on. I take Your hand so You will guide my steps. You want me to be fearless and not fearful in these days ahead. Thank You for conquering sin and death by Your sacrifice of love through Jesus Christ. There is nothing for me to fear when I trust You. Nothing is too hard for You, my Lord and Savior! I am holding Your hand and my fear is gone. I am drinking of Your living water so I will not be thirsty again! Eternal life is mine in You. I love You eternally!

In Jesus name,
Amen

November 7

His Promise

"When they saw the star, they rejoiced exceedingly with great joy."
Matthew 2:10

My Prayer

Dear Heavenly Father,

Thank You for the joy that You bring me! I am rejoicing as I see the light of Your enduring love. You have given me great hope because of who you are. As I look up, I see You and feel Your overwhelming power and utmost joy. It is so good to know You, my Lord! Thank You for shining Your light upon me as I see You, my promised Savior, now and forevermore!

In Jesus' name,
Amen

November 8

"Let the word of God dwell in you richly, teaching and admonishing one another in all wisdom, singing psalms and hymns and spiritual songs, with thankfulness in your hearts to God."
Colossians 3:16

My Prayer

Dear Heavenly Father,

Thank You for showing me the way when I follow You. Because I trust You, Lord, I know which way to go. You have greater blessings in store me as I let Your Word dwell in me. As I listen and obey You, I will be greatly enriched. Your Word gives me direction and guidance. Your love encourages and comforts me. Your peace rules in me. Your joy overwhelms me and I am praising You. I am letting go and letting You work mightily in me!

In Jesus' name,
Amen

November 9

"The LORD is good to those who wait for him,
to the soul who seeks him."
Lamentations 3:25

My Prayer

Dear Heavenly Father,

I will wait for You, Lord! I know that You will be good to me as I seek You more and more. Peace and courage come to me as I wait for You. Only You can give me the strength to press on as I wait upon You. I will not get impatient, but I will trust You in the waiting. Your timing is always perfect. I am seeking You with all my soul!

In Jesus' name,
Amen

November 10

His Promise

May mercy, and peace, and love be multiplied to you."
Jude 1:2

My Prayer

Dear Heavenly Father,

Oh, how I want more mercy, peace, and love. You will multiply all of these in my life as I trust You more. You provide me with more than I could ever ask for when I wholeheartedly and steadfastly seek You. I am stronger and can endure as I come closer to You. My strength grows when my focus is upon You. In your presence is fullness of peace and joy. At Your right hand, I find mercy and grace, forevermore!

In Jesus' name,
Amen

November 11

"Now you, brothers, like Isaac, are children of promise."
Galatians 4:28

My Prayer

Dear Heavenly Father,

Thank You for Your promises that are real for me today. I believe Your promises to me, and I thank You for the relationship I have with You. I am filled with hope when I listen with my heart and actively walk by faith. You are so good to me, my Lord! Your grace, goodness, and mercy reign in my life because I have made You Lord of my life. Thank You for watching over me! I love You, my Lord!

In Jesus' name,
Amen

November 12

His Promise

*"And the Word became flesh and dwelt among us,
and we have seen his glory, glory as of the only Son
from the Father, full of grace and truth."*
John 1:14

My Prayer

Dear Heavenly Father,

You are dwelling among me, Lord, because of Your Holy Spirit inside me. I am so graced and humbled by Your mighty presence in and around me! Thank You for letting me see Your glory as You live in me. I know Your Word will grow within me as I remain close to You and dwell with You. I see with eyes of grace as I see Your glory!

In Jesus' name,
Amen

November 13

His Promise

*"For God gave us a spirit not of fear but of power
and love and self-control."*
2 Timothy 1:7

My Prayer

Dear Heavenly Father,

I know You will give me a Spirit of power, love, and
self-control as I keep drawing closer to You. Thank
You for erasing all my fears as I trust You more each
day. I am basking in the goodness of Your glory!
Every day is more precious to me as I am more
devoted to You. I can see Your love all around me
and I am full of devoted love to You, my Lord!

In Jesus' name,
Amen

November 14

"Where your treasure is, there will your heart be also."
Luke 12:34

My Prayer

Dear Heavenly Father,

Thank You for being my treasure. My heart is with You always. I am so thankful for everything You have done for me! My heart is rejoicing for who You are to me! I love You so much, my Lord! Your love for me has no end and lives eternally in me! I am fully devoted to You, my Lord, my treasure, now and forevermore!

In Jesus name,
Amen

November 15

His Promise

*"Rejoice in the Lord always; again I will say,
rejoice!"*
Philippians 4:4

My Prayer

Dear Heavenly Father,

I am rejoicing because You are my Lord! Again and
again, I will rejoice for You because You are my
Lord and Savior! I am so thankful for You and Your
love for me! Every day is special because I am filled
with Your utmost joy! I will keep rejoicing in You
and being thankful. It is so good to be resting in Your
arms. I give You all the glory for the joy that is in me!
You are so amazing, Lord! I will rejoice and rejoice!

In Jesus' name,
Amen

329

November 16

His Promise

"And so, from the day we heard, we have not ceased to pray for you asking that you may be filled with the knowledge of his will in all spiritual wisdom and understanding."
Colossians 1:9

My Prayer

Dear Heavenly Father,

I am praying to see clearer with spiritual eyes of faith. Thank You for opening my eyes to see what you see. I am so thankful to have You in my life! I can only see what you see when I focus on You and Your steadfast love for me. I want to live with eyes of faith and draw closer to You. Every day I see more opportunities to live in love with those around me. Thank You for putting these "just in time moments" in front of me so I can be close to You.

In Jesus' name,
Amen

November 17

"You make known to me the path of life; in your presence there is fullness of joy;at your right hand are pleasures forevermore."
Psalm 16:11

My Prayer

Dear Heavenly Father,

Your joy is in me! My joy is full because I have You living in me! Thank You for putting Your Spirit deep down in my soul. I am so full of the wonderment of who You are to me. Your glory fills my heart and blesses my soul. My life is filled with abundant joy knowing You are taking care of me. You are there in the smallest details and in the biggest challenges. I will worship You all the days of my life! My joy will never leave because You live in me!

In Jesus' name,
Amen

November 18

"If the Spirit of him who raised Jesus from the dead dwells in you, he who raised Christ Jesus from the dead will also give life to your mortal bodies through his Spirit who dwells in you."
Romans 8:11

My Prayer

Dear Heavenly Father,

You are so wonderful! I know You want me to set my mind on the Spirit so that I can have life and peace. I will look to You and ponder Your goodness and glory! Thank You for giving me life! I am basking in the peace that comes from fully trusting You and centering my life on You. I am amazed and humbled that the same Spirit that rose Jesus from death to life lives inside me! Thank You for helping me to focus on my new life in You as I let the Spirit lead me! I am living an abundant life with You in me!

In Jesus' name,
Amen

November 19

His Promise

"Ask, and it will be given to you; seek, and you will find; knock, and it will be opened to you."
Matthew 7:7

My Prayer

Dear Heavenly Father,

Oh, how I love You Lord! I am asking by faith for what is on my heart today. I know that You love to answer me and that You want me to pray faithfully. Help me to trust You and lean into You more and more. I will be waiting patiently as I pray. I will keep patiently believing. I know that if I keep seeking, You will answer and open the door for me!

In Jesus' name,
Amen

November 20

His Promise

*"Though I walk in the midst of trouble, you preserve
my life; you stretch out your hand against the wrath
of my enemies and your right hand delivers me."*
Psalm 138:7

My Prayer

Dear Heavenly Father,

I know when I need protection, You are there. I am
basking in Your goodness and glory! Your promises
to securely guide me and keep me safe are real. You
hem me in before and behind with Your hand upon
me. You are my stronghold and stability. I need You,
Lord, to hold me as I wait patiently upon You. You
will always show up for me with open arms! I am
opening my heart to You and am resting in Your
promises to keep me safe and secure, now and
forevermore!

In Jesus' name,
Amen

November 21

His Promise

*"You shall worship the Lord your God,
and him only shall you serve."*
Luke 4:8

My Prayer

Dear Heavenly Father,

Thank You for helping me when I seek Your guidance. I will listen to You and act obediently. As I worship You, there is greater hope! I am so excited to share my heart with You and worship You in Spirit and in Truth. You have given me peace as I am present in Your presence. There is fullness of joy where You are! All my days are filled with purpose when my heart is close to You. Thank You for showing me the way to life which exists through You. I am basking in Your goodness and Your glory as I serve You!

In Jesus' name,
Amen

November 22

His Promise

"If you are not firm in faith, you will not be firm at all."
Isaiah 7:9

My Prayer

Dear Heavenly Father,

I will stand firm in my faith as I stand with You. I know You are giving me strength as I come closer to Your love. I am more devoted to You every day. Even in these crazy and challenging days, I feel encouraged. My faith has increased as I spend time with You in prayer and meditation of Your Word. Thank You for answering my prayers! I stand stronger when I stand firm in my faith. There is no other way to stand except with You, my Lord. You are always faithful!

In Jesus' name,
Amen

November 23

His Promise

"So if the Son sets you free, you will be free indeed."
John 8:36

My Prayer

Dear Heavenly Father,

You are mighty to save me, Lord! Your grace has set me free! As I cast my burdens onto You, I am sustained. Thank You for this promise that encourages my soul. In Your arms, I find freedom. As I let go of my worry, You bring me peace and calmness. In Your presence, there is hope and fullness of joy! I am free, indeed, as I let You work in me again and again!

In Jesus' name,
Amen

November 24

"Guide our feet into the way of peace."
Luke 1:79

My Prayer

Dear Heavenly Father,

You are my peace. In the stillness of my soul, You are there guiding and directing me as I let go and let You work in me. I will draw to You more in the moments I am anxious and restless. Your perfect peace is present when I am still. I know You want me to be calm and trust You in all circumstances even when I do not understand. As I do, You will direct my path and guide my feet in the way of peace. Thank You for comforting my soul by bringing me peace!

In Jesus' name,
Amen

November 25

"Be still before the LORD and wait patiently for him;
fret not yourself over the one who prospers in his
way, over the man who carries out evil devices!"
Psalm 37:7

My Prayer

Dear Heavenly Father,

I will be still and wait for You. In the stillness of my soul, You are there. When I need You, all I need do is ask and You show up for me. Thank You for attending to the voice of my prayers. I know Your response is just a prayer away for me. Your timing is always perfect. I trust You more with each prayer I pray. I am hopeful for what I believe even when I do not see. I wait patiently for You, Lord. You bring me to a perfect place of peace as I still myself before You!

In Jesus' name,
Amen

November 26

"Weeping may tarry for the night,
but joy comes with the morning."
Psalm 30:5

My Prayer

Dear Heavenly Father,

You see my tears and know my fears. When I weep, You comfort me with Your presence. When I struggle, You give me hope by Your grace. When I am afraid, You give me more faith to press on with You. My weeping turns to joy when You come to me. My joy is present because You are present in me. Thank You for giving me fullness of utmost joy! I am basking in the joy that is mine in You. I trust You completely with my whole heart and soul!

In Jesus' name,
Amen

November 27

His Promise

*"My grace is sufficient for you,
for my power is made perfect in weakness."*
2 Corinthians 12:9

My Prayer

Dear Heavenly Father,

Oh, how I need Your grace! You know the deepest needs of my soul and have given me Your abundant grace. You lavish grace upon my life! For when I am weak, Your power brings life into me. I am made perfect in my weakness only through You, and I have strength because You have empowered me. In Your presence, I am strong and brave for the challenges before me. Thank You, Lord, for this promise of grace that comforts me and fills me full of greater hope for what lies ahead. Your grace is sufficient for me!

In Jesus' name,
Amen

November 28

His Promise

"Brothers, I do not consider that I have made it my own. But one thing I do: forgetting what lies behind and straining forward to what lies ahead."
Philippians 3:13

My Prayer

Dear Heavenly Father,

Thank You for helping me press forward to what lies ahead. I am hopeful for what I know is mine in You as I keep pressing on in faith. My goal is to be closer to You and I will keep my focus on You, my prize! In You, there is fullness of joy, now and life everlasting! I have moved forward with Your leading and encouragement. I know that all things will work out for good to bring You glory! You have revealed Your promises to me, and I am grateful and humbled by Your goodness and mercy that is mine through You!

In Jesus' name,
Amen

November 29

His Promise

"Again I say to you, if two of you agree on earth, about anything they ask, it will be done for them by my Father in heaven."
Matthew 18:19

My Prayer

Dear Heavenly Father,

I have hope that is alive in You, my Lord, even in uncertain times. Thank You for this new hope You give me each day. As I hope in You, I will keep rejoicing! My hope continues to grow as I grow closer to You, my Lord. I will be patient as I trust You more and more because You are showing me great and mighty things that You want for me. I will constantly pray for what is on my heart. I will never give up praying! Thank You for tuning in to the voice of my prayers and answering my requests lifted to You, my living hope! I love You!

In Jesus' name,
Amen

November 30

*"I will give thanks to the LORD with my whole heart;
I will recount all of your wonderful deeds."
Psalm 9:1*

My Prayer

Dear Heavenly Father,

Oh, how wonderful You are to me, my
Lord! You are ever present in my life as I
have made You my Lord and Savior. I
am grateful and incredibly blessed by
Your amazing grace and eternal love!
Thank You for all the blessings
bestowed upon me, starting with my
relationship with You! I need You in
my life every day and in all ways. I
will faithfully pursue You as I ponder
my blessings today and remain thankful all
the days of my life!

In Jesus' name,
Amen

Rejoice in hope, be patient in tribulation, be constant in prayer.

ROMANS 12:12

December 1

"For nothing will be impossible with God."
Luke 1:37

My Prayer

Dear Heavenly Father,

I am so thankful You honor Your Word and do what You say You will do! There is never a question as to if You will act on my behalf. I believe You because You are always faithful! Nothing is impossible for You! All the desires of my heart are possible for You when I choose to believe! Your will is best. You see the whole plan. You know how all things will work out. My role is to trust You and believe by never letting doubt or unbelief settle in my heart. I am letting go and keeping my faith for greater days ahead. You give me purpose and passion to press on with faith-filled prayers!

In Jesus' name,
Amen

December 2

*"God is our refuge and strength,
a very present help in trouble."*
Psalm 46:1

My Prayer

Dear Heavenly Father,

Oh, how I thank You for giving me courage and for strengthening me! I love knowing that when I face trouble, You will be there to give me extra endurance and strength. I believe You will help me whenever I come to You and find my rest and refuge in You. You are there as I reach out and hold Your hand. Thank You for giving me hope when I cling to Your promises. I will not fear when You are here with me. My refuge is in You, my Lord, and I am strong in Your mighty presence!

In Jesus' name,
Amen

December 3

His Promise

*"Satisfy us in the morning with your steadfast love,
that we may rejoice and be glad all our days."*
Psalm 90:14

My Prayer

Dear Heavenly Father,

Oh, how I thank You, Lord, for Your steadfast love!
You are so loving and faithful, and I am in awe of
Your power and glory! You speak and mountains
move. You listen to my prayers and answer me. You
make things happen so that Your will can be done in
Your perfect timing. You have touched my heart with
power and purpose, Lord, and I am praising You for
all that You are to me! I will keep
abiding in Your love and
obeying Your commands to
love others so that You will
know how much I love You!

In Jesus' name,
Amen

December 4

"You also must be ready, for the Son of Man is coming at an hour you do not expect."
Matthew 24:44

My Prayer

Dear Heavenly Father,

You tell me to be ready for Your return. Only You know when that promise will be fulfilled. I wait with hope knowing that my present and my future are full of life in You because I have made You my Lord. As I wait, I will worship and trust You. As I trust You more, I will serve You faithfully and wholeheartedly. I am prepared because I have given You all my heart and made my home in You! I am secure because I have surrendered all to You, Christ Jesus! All of Your promises have their *yes* in You! I pray that we are all made ready and prepared for Your return!

In Jesus' name,
Amen

December 5

His Promise

"May the LORD bless you from Zion,
he who made heaven and earth!"
Psalm 134:3

My Prayer

Dear Heavenly Father,

Oh, how I praise You, Lord! You are Holy and I worship Your majesty! There are blessings You give me that flow from my blessed relationship with You. I have Your promised blessings as I fully trust and follow You. Thank You for bringing me hope as I pray this promise that comes from You. I am devoted to You, and I will seek You with all my heart, my Lord and Savior, forever!

In Jesus' name,
Amen

December 6

His Promise

*"Restore us again, O God of our salvation, and put
away your indignation toward us!"*
Psalm 85:4

My Prayer

Dear Heavenly Father,

I know that You will restore me to my salvation as I
continue pressing forward with You. I have been
walking by faith one step at a time, one day at a time,
but there are still challenges tugging at my heart. You
see my heart and know my every thought. I am never
alone because You are always present in me. I have
trusted You as my Lord and first love. Thank You for
restoring me to that place of joy with You. I will let
go and be still to find the promised peace that only
You bring! Revive me, Lord!

In Jesus' name,
Amen

December 7

"The heart of man plans his way,
but the LORD establishes his steps."
Proverbs 16:9

My Prayer

Dear Heavenly Father,

Thank You for giving me direction as I let go and let You work in me. You have the perfect plan for me that will be established in my life when I let go of control and let You show me the way. You have brought me such joy as I keep in step with You one step at a time! I see clearly with Your eyes and feel comforted by Your love for me. Your promises give me new joy and greater hope as I cling to You!

In Jesus' name,
Amen

December 8

His Promise

"Have I not commanded you? Be strong and courageous. Do not be frightened, and do not be dismayed, of the LORD your God is with you wherever you go."
Joshua 1:9

My Prayer

Dear Heavenly Father,

I give You my fears and hold on to Your hand. I will not fear when You are here with me. You lead me where I need to go with eyes to see and arms wide open to receive Your love. It is in Your presence that I feel the fullness of Your sweet joy. Where You are is where I want to be! There is no fear, but only peace, as I walk hand in hand with You. As I live by faith with Your goodness and glory, I am fearless and free in You, my Rescuer and Redeemer, forever!

In Jesus' name,
Amen

December 9

"My brothers, show no partiality as you hold the faith in our Lord Jesus Christ, the Lord of glory."
James 2:1

My Prayer

Dear Heavenly Father,

I know You are asking me to look to You for guidance. I can easily be led astray and influenced by others, but You say to keep my faith fixed firmly on You. I am not focusing on the world and its ways of bias and judgment any longer, Lord. I am keeping my gaze on Your ways more and more each day so that You can show me the direction I need to go. I will put faith first and let my fear of what might happen disappear. Thank You, Lord, for guiding me into all truth. I am holding onto faith in You, my Lord and Savior!

In   Jesus' name,
Amen

December 10

*"Trust in him at all times, O people, pour out your
heart before him; God is a refuge for us."*
Psalm 62:8

My Prayer

Dear Heavenly Father,

I know You want me to draw closer to You. I am
pouring out my heart before You, Lord, and I hear
You calling me to trust You. Even when I cannot see,
You are working out the details of my life. As I let
go, my soul is satisfied knowing You are with me. I
will pray as I exhale and inhale Your love. You are so
close to my heart, Lord, as I live by the heartbeat of
Your Spirit deep within me. As I am still in Your
presence, my faith grows deeper, and I am completely
at peace.

In Jesus' name,
Amen

December 11

His Promise

*"Wait for the LORD be strong, and let your heart
take courage, wait for the Lord!"*
Psalm 27:14

My Prayer

Dear Heavenly Father,

I am waiting on You, Lord, with my heart open and
close to yours as I pray. I need courage to face the
challenges today. I know that as I patiently wait for
You to act, You are infusing me with more power. I
am listening to Your voice guiding me on the right
path. I will not give up as I wait but will continue
obeying You to find strength. As I let go of my fears,
I will grow closer to Your love. I am full of hope and
courage as I cling tighter to Your promises! My faith
has come to life in You!

In Jesus' name,
Amen

December 12

"Now the Lord is the Spirit, and where the Spirit of the Lord is, there is freedom."
2 Corinthians 3:17

My Prayer

Dear Heavenly Father,

As I pray to You today, I want to start by telling You how much I love You! Because of my relationship with You, I have joy that has settled deep within me. I know that Your hand is always upon me and I feel safe and secure. It is so good to be right in the center of Your love where I am free. You hem me in behind and before and there is no other place I would rather be. There is freedom where You reign! Thank You for Your Spirit that lives in me. Where the Spirit of the Lord reigns, there is freedom, indeed! I am grateful and blessed and humbly thankful for You, my Lord and Savior forever!

In Jesus' name,
Amen

December 13

"Now to him who is able to do far more abundantly than all we ask or think, according to the power at work in us, to him be the glory in the church and in Christ Jesus throughout all generations, forever and ever. Amen."
Ephesians 3:20-21

My Prayer

Dear Heavenly Father,

You can do more in me as I trust You. Help me to let go of my doubt and fear and let You work mightily and powerfully in me. As I surrender all, You will do far abundantly more in me. As I let You work in me, You will work things out for my good and Your glory. Help me draw to You and shine the light of Your love so that others can see You. I am forever strengthened with Your presence in my life, my Lord. You are my all in all!

In Jesus' name,
Amen

December 14

"Now may our Lord Jesus Christ himself, and God our Father, who loved us and gave us eternal comfort and good hope through grace, comfort your hearts and establish them in every good work and word."
2 Thessalonians 2:16-17

My Prayer

Dear Heavenly Father,

Oh, how I love You! I know that You are working in me for Your will and good pleasure. Help me to continue drawing to You as I let go and let You work in me. There are days where my faith is tested, and I want to be found faithful in Your sight. I will trust You and keep going in the direction You are leading me. I will not give up but will find comfort with Your hand upon me. I need You, Lord, to give me strength to finish this race before me. I will stay close to You and let my faith take me to new spiritual heights where You are leading and strengthening me for the journey. There is joy in this journey with You, Lord!

In Jesus' name,
Amen

December 15

"Save us, O LORD our God, and gather us from among the nations, that we may give thanks to your holy name and glory in your praise."
Psalm 106:47

My Prayer

Dear Heavenly Father,

Oh, how we need You to save us all! We know you promise salvation for all who believe! We pray for those who do not know You to come to You and give You their hearts. We pray for salvation for the lost. We pray for redemption for those who need Your touch. We ask for healing to come to those in pain. We seek peace and joy in the midst of sorrow. We ask for revival to come to all of us. We believe Your promises and have set our hope in You as we pray. Lord, come save and revive us!

In Jesus' name,
Amen

December 16

"For he will hide me in his shelter in the day of trouble; he will conceal me under the cover of his tent; he will lift me high upon a rock."
Psalm 27:5

My Prayer

Dear Heavenly Father,

Thank You for setting me free! With You I have salvation and strength to press on. When I am weak, You are strong and lift me higher! Help me to be close to Your voice of Truth as I listen to You. I can hear You when I draw closer to Your love. It is in the stillness of my soul where I feel You and am awakened to new life in Christ. Help me, Lord, to do what You have called me to do. I have found peace as I trust and obey You. In Your presence there is eternal perfect peace and fullness of great joy for me!

In Jesus' name,
Amen

December 17

"A new commandment I give to you, that you love one another: just as I have loved you, you also are to love one another."
John 13:34

My Prayer

Dear Heavenly Father,

I will share my love with others as You have asked me, Lord. It is so good to love as You have loved! You shine Your love upon me and help me feel encouraged as I reach out to love with Your love. It is so special to be able to live in the light of Your love! As I love You, I am enlightened with the love You share and counsel. As I love others, You will enrich my life with hope and encircle my life with peace. Loving others is a special gift that I can receive and share. So thankful to be able to live in love with You, my Lord!

In Jesus' name,
Amen

December 18

"Jesus said to him, 'I am the way, and the truth, and the life. No one comes to the Father except through me.'"
John 14:7

My Prayer

Dear Heavenly Father,

I will not be afraid because You are the Way, the Truth, and the Life. You have given me strength and courage to face each challenge. I am stronger each day as I let You lead me. I will not let fear have a hold over me anymore because I am living fearlessly with You. There is nothing that can stop me from living in this freedom when I am close to You. I am saying goodbye to fear and doubt and hello to my new way of living in joy and peace. With You, my Defender, I know all things are possible! There is no more fear!

In Jesus' name,
Amen

December 19

"Peace be with you."
John 20:19

My Prayer

Dear Heavenly Father,

I need Your peace to rest on me. I need You, Lord, my Prince of Peace. In these restless and challenging times, I can rely on Your perfect peace. I trust You, my Lord, and know You will grow my faith as I experience You daily. You are the Bread of Life who promises to give me all that I need as I come closer to You and stay devoted to You. I will lean on You to find comfort for my weary soul and broken heart. Only You can rescue and restore me to a place of contentment and security. Peace be still, my soul!

In Jesus' name,
Amen

December 20

His Promise

"I can do all things through him who strengthens me."
Philippians 4:13

My Prayer

Dear Heavenly Father,

Thank You for strengthening me, my Lord. You ask me to let go of control and trust You for all that I need. You will make a way through these difficult situations and problems I am facing. I will open my heart to do all that You are telling me. As I listen, I hear Your truth and my courage to obey increases greatly, even in the face of adversity. I am infused with power from You as I walk by faith. You promise to strengthen me so that You can work in and through me. Give me this day my daily bread. I need all that You promise, Lord!

In Jesus' name,
Amen

December 21

"And all who believed were together and had all things in common."
Acts 2:44

My Prayer

Dear Heavenly Father,

It is so good to come together as one to pray and worship You! When we seek You with one heart, mind, and soul, we have pure joy and come closer to Your love. As we love You, we have the hunger and passion that comes alive and grows in our souls. I am eager to see what You will do in hearts that put You first. I know that only You can change hardened hearts and soften them. I will keep seeking revival for all as I pray and worship You, my Lord! I want to please You and live for You with Your abundance of joy spilling over in me!

In Jesus' name,
Amen

December 22

"Rejoice always, pray without ceasing, give thanks in all circumstances; for this is the will of God in Christ Jesus for you."
1 Thessalonians 5:16-18

My Prayer

Dear Heavenly Father,

I know You hear me when I pray. I will pray with a thankful heart believing that You will answer me. You wait for me to speak to You with faith in my soul and praise on my lips. I will pray with eager anticipation of seeing Your promises come to life. You speak and I will listen, Lord. I hear Your beautiful voice encouraging me as you say, "I love you dear child." Oh, how you know I need to hear this all the time! I will show my love and gratitude for this enriching relationship I have with You as I keep Your commandments and Your joy deep in my heart, soul, and mind! I love You!

In Jesus' name,
Amen

December 23

"Oh, magnify the LORD with me,
and let us exalt his name together!"
Psalm 34:3

My Prayer

Dear Heavenly Father,

I will praise You! I will magnify Your glorious name forever because You are mighty, all powerful, and magnificent! Your love has touched my heart and I am praising You for the endless joy You bring me! My heart is full of hope as I pray and ponder the glory only You can bring to all! Thank You for giving us Jesus who loves unconditionally. He has saved us all by grace which has been lavished upon us so richly. When we believe, we receive a glorious inheritance with You, our Father, through Jesus. Thank You for richly blessing my life with my Savior, Jesus Christ! I do believe!

In Jesus' name,
Amen

December 24

His Promise

*"My soul magnifies the Lord, and my spirit rejoices
in God my Savior."*
Luke 1:46

My Prayer

Dear Heavenly Father,

You are so wonderful, and I am in awe of Your
wonder and glory! I am truly blessed to be one of
Your children living in Your presence, my Lord! You
have richly blessed my life and I live
fully engaged with the fire of Your
Spirit dwelling within me. I am
praying for healing and
wholeness that only You can
bring to me and those I am lifting
up in prayer. I am sure of what
You promise me as I stay faithful and fearless.
Nothing can stop me from leaning closer to Your love
and mercy! This I know: I am saved by grace to live
in love. My joy is found in You, my Lord and Savior!

In Jesus' name,
Amen

December 25

"And suddenly there was with the angel a multitude
of the heavenly host praising God and saying,
'Glory to God in the highest, and on earth peace
among those with whom he is pleased!"
Luke 2:13-14

My Prayer

Dear Heavenly Father,

Oh, how thankful I am for You! In Your presence is fullness of joy and present peace. I know all Your promises are true as You speak life over me. I have greater faith as I lean closer to You. My eyes see Your hand upon the circumstances of my life in miraculous ways and I am in awe of Your wonder. I hear You speak mercy over me to wipe away my doubt and fear and it is well with my soul. I have faith and have experienced hope when You pour Your bountiful blessings of love over me. I am praising You, O Lord, my God, with a thankful heart for giving me Jesus as my Savior! How I love to praise You and remember all that You have promised me yesterday, today, and tomorrow. Everything is possible for You! Yes, I do believe!

In Jesus' name,
Amen

December 26

"The LORD is my shepherd, I shall not want."
Psalm 23:1

My Prayer

Dear Heavenly Father,

I praise You for who You are and how much You love me. You lift me up and give me strength and faith even in the most difficult times. You offer rest and comfort as I lean in on You. I can see Your hand of mercy all around me when I am close to You. I am alive with new faith as I have You present in my life. Your powerful presence gives me hope and I can live with new joy as I live connected to You. I have no fear when you are near. I am confident and content, Lord, as You are my Shepherd! You are my all in all and I have everything I need in You!

In Jesus' name,
Amen

December 27

His Promise

"Every good gift and every perfect gift is from above, coming down from the Father of lights with whom there is no variation or shadow due to change."
James 1:17

My Prayer

Dear Heavenly Father,

How wonderful are Your promises to me, O Lord! You are faithful with Your beautiful gifts of love. I see You and Your promises as I look to the light. I believe You are the same, never changing, and always giving me new hope. I am thankful for Your gift of grace that You lavish so generously over me. I am eagerly and patiently waiting to see what Your will is for me. Thank You for opening the eyes of my heart to see Your light. Everywhere I look, I see You and know You are working things out for good. I will keep singing my praises to You, my Lord, my Miracle Worker and Promise Keeper!

In Jesus' name,
Amen

December 28

His Promise

"Brothers, I do not consider that I have made it on my own. But one thing I do: forgetting what lies behind and straining forward to what lies ahead. I press on toward the goal for the prize of the upward call of God in Christ Jesus."
Philippians 3:13-14

My Prayer

Dear Heavenly Father,

I will press on towards the prize of my calling in You, My Lord. In these days of uncertainty, I am certain of Your love and grace upon me. I will dedicate my life to You so that You can move in me and grow my passion and hunger for You. My sustenance is found in You and not in the things of this world. As I put my faith in You, my faithful Father, You will bless me with new life in Christ! You have given me Jesus, the Bread of Life! I will strain forward to what lies ahead as I choose the upward call of God in Christ Jesus. I cling tightly to You, Lord, my best portion!

In Jesus' name,
Amen

December 29

"He must increase, but I must decrease."
John 3:30

My Prayer

Dear Heavenly Father,

I know You want me to put You first so You can increase Your presence in my life. Your joy will grow inside of me as I let go of self and let You direct my steps. As I commit my way to You, I know You will act. As I lean in closer, the desires of my heart become clearer. I seek to grow my relationship with You, my Lord. You will increase as I let go and decrease. You will be my first thought and my whole portion. As I lean on You and trust You more, I will find healing and wholeness because You promise to give me strength. I will seek after You, my Lord, with a devoted and joyful heart so that I can be enlightened with hope!

In Jesus' name,
Amen

December 30

His Promise

"Cast your burden on the LORD,
and he will sustain you; he will never permit the
righteous to be moved."
Psalm 55:22

My Prayer

Dear Heavenly Father,

I know You will sustain me as I cast my burdens onto You. I am eager to see how You will make a way for me when there seems to be no way. I know You are able! Thank You for showing me how I can be free from burden when I let go and trust You! As I commit my way to You, I know You will act. I have seen You do that for me before, and I am certain You will do it again! What a joy it is to know You love me so much that You will take all my cares and concerns and free me of them. I am blessed, indeed!

In Jesus' name,
Amen

December 31

"Trust in the LORD with all your heart, and do not lean on your own understanding. In all your ways acknowledge him, and he will make straight your paths."
Proverbs 3:5-6

My Prayer

Dear Heavenly Father,

You can do more in me when I trust You. Help me to let go of my doubt and fear and let You work mightily and powerfully in me. As I surrender all, You will do great works within me. As I let You transform me, You will work things out for my good and Your glory. Help me draw to You and shine the light of Your love so that others can see You. I am forever strengthened with Your presence in my life, my Lord. You are my all in all and I do trust You with all my heart!

In Jesus' name,
Amen

Also By Jill Lowry

The Inspirational Devotions Collection

Available on Amazon

Finding Joy in Jesus
https://www.amazon.com/dp/B079VTNMY9

Hearts on Fire
https://www.amazon.com/dp/B07HKK2MN9

Be Still
https://www.amazon.com/dp/B08LTRBDN5

Discover how you can have the second touch of Jesus alive in you.

Available on Amazon
https://www.amazon.com/dp/B093XY7HPZ

Looking for More?

God-Size Your Prayers to Find Your Destiny

Available on Amazon
https://www.amazon.com/dp/B07TW7YMHV

Prayer Journals also Available on Amazon

https://www.amazon.com/dp/1693027763

https://www.amazon.com/dp/0578633906

Jill Lowry

Women's Ministry Event?

Need a keynote speaker?

Contact Jill.

Simply head to her website and fill out the contact form with your contact info, information about your event, and the dates of your event.

Inspire ♥ Encourage ♥ Uplift

https://www.jilllowryministries.com/contact

ABOUT THE AUTHOR

Jill Lowry is an ardent follower of Jesus who has a desire and passion to communicate His truth. Inspired by the Holy Spirit, her writings combine the accuracy of a scholar with the practicality of a wife and mother. Jill grew up in San Antonio, Texas. She graduated from the University of Texas with a Bachelor of Business Administration in Marketing and holds a law degree from St. Mary's University School of Law.

Jill is the founder and president of a student mentoring and food program, Mt Vernon Cares, created for at-risk students at the local Junior High and High School. She is one of the hosts of a faith-based weekly radio talk show and podcast, Real Life Real People Radio. She also co-hosts another podcast, Journey with Jesus, where two friends share truths and positivity about how to find joy in Jesus. In addition, Jill is a contributing partner on Bible.com where you can read more of her devotionals.

Jill takes every opportunity to pray with friends and neighbors in need and considers intercessory prayer a vital part of her ministry. She is part of a weekly community prayer group which meets on the Downtown Square to pray for revival in her community and beyond.

Visit her website for more information on these ministries and subscribe to receive inspirational daily prayers.

http://www.jilllowryministries.com

Made in United States
Orlando, FL
09 January 2022

13209077R00215